Interface Vol 11 No 2/2008

Church in China

Contents

Interface Vol 11 No 2/2008

Introduction

Paul Rule

Paul Rule
Melbourne

China has been a challenge to Christianity since the beginning of modern times and it remains so today. Here is a great civilisation comprising a quarter of humankind, yet largely untouched by Christian values and beliefs. Any theological evaluation of the state of world Christianity that does not take China into account is impoverished and radically incomplete.

Of course, there have been some Christians in China, probably for nearly as long as Christianity has existed, and today there may be as many as fifty to eighty million; the very fact that nobody can count them says much about their low public profile. However, there is much to learn from the history of the previous four 'encounters' of

Christianity with China, an account of which is given in this issue by Jeroom Heyndrickx who has himself played a not inconsiderable role in the fifth.

Most of the contributions to this China issue of *Interface* deal with the last twenty years, a period marked by the development of what has been called 'Sino-theology' (see Gianni Criveller's account of this development). Although this movement began in the seventeenth century, it was largely stillborn and even today, contemporary Chinese churches are too busy surviving and consolidating to give the enterprise the attention it deserves. Support is needed from sympathetic Christian theologians and scholars outside the People's Republic of China, including but not exclusively those of the Chinese diaspora.

The contents of this issue have inevitably but not intentionally a Catholic bias since the editor is a historian of the Catholic Church in China, but much of the discussion is applicable to the wider Chinese Christian church. Justin Tan's contribution to this issue discusses divisions in the Protestant churches similar to and deriving from much the same forces as the divisions in the Chinese Catholic Church. Despite the Chinese government's divisive tactic of regarding the Tianzhu Jiao (Catholicism) administratively as a totally different religion from the Jidu Jiao (Protestant Christianity), there are signs of ecumenical rapprochement at the local and national levels.

Recently formal discussions began in Shanghai between Chinese Christians and Chinese Muslims. As a result a younger generation of religious leaders seems intent on reopening an inter-religious dialogue, one that had hardly begun after World War II before it was interrupted by the anti-religious campaigns of the Communist Revolution. The case of Buddhism is discussed here by Benoît Vermander, a Jesuit anthropologist stationed in Taiwan, who describes the revival or awakening of Chinese Buddhism since the Cultural Revolution. He makes the interesting suggestion that state control of religion has had the paradoxical effect of creating a new interdependence among Chinese Buddhists. Perhaps the same may prove true of Chinese religion in general.

While the much-lauded Jesuit interaction between Christianity and Confucianism from the time of Matteo Ricci (in China 1583–1610) is well known, it is only in recent times that a similar interaction in theology and spirituality between Chinese Buddhism and Daoism has occurred. The late Yves Raguin SJ[1] has shown how an approach through spirituality can overcome apparent doctrinal divides.

Similarly, in the last years of his life, the Cistercian monk, Thomas Merton, struggled to overcome the words that divide us:

> There are so many words that one cannot get to God as long as He is thought to be on the side of the words. But when he is placed firmly beyond the other side of words, the words multiply like flies and there is a great buzzing religion, very profitable, very holy, very spurious.[2]

1. Yves Raguin SJ, *Ways of Contemplation East and West*, 4 volumes (Taipei: Ricci Institute, 1993–2001).
2. Thomas Merton, letter of 1965, in *The Courage for Truth: the Letters*

Before his tragic accidental death in Thailand Merton was discovering, in his contacts with monks of many traditions, ways to overcome these barriers through commonality of religious experience and religion-inspired social activism.

The moral and spiritual vacuum that has followed the extraordinary economic progress of China in recent years has had the paradoxical effect of producing what the government labels a 'religious fever'. Roderick O'Brien and Claudia Devaux, who have spent various periods teaching in China, reflect in this issue on some of its manifestations. Although little known outside China, this religious revival may hold lessons for all of us. It seeks alternatives to the 'greed is good' values of global capitalism and the heartlessness of a society based on it. Emerging from it are some extremely interesting ideas, from which theologians throughout the Christian world might profit. A popular Italian comedy film of the era when Maoism was all the rage in the West was entitled *China is Near*. China is still near if only we bother to look hard at it and learn from it.

of Thomas Merton to Writers, edited by Christine M Bochen (New York: Farrar, Strauss, Giroux, 1993), 225.

Interface Vol 11 No 2/2008

Chapter One

Christian Studies in China

Gianni Criveller

Gianni Criveller

The story of the relationship between Christianity and China is a long one (about 1500 years long!), a story of trial and error, of attempts, partial successes, failures and new beginnings. The last decade of the twentieth century seemed to mark one of these new beginnings. The emergence of a peculiar phenomenon in Chinese academia, namely 'Christian Studies', and a group of scholars called 'cultural Christians', sparked hope of a new cultural season for Christianity in China, a renewed hope for an inculturated Christianity, or more specifically for an inculturated theology. As London-based China watcher, Edmond Tang, says: 'It is my conviction that never before in recent Chinese history, since the time of Matteo Ricci, has Chinese society been as open to Christianity as today.'

Is there a new chance for Christianity to play a significant role in Chinese society and culture? Will there be the
development of a truly Chinese Christianity, or a Chinese
Christian theology? The phenomenon of Christian studies in China, as they have evolved since the early 1990s,
can offer clues to answering these questions.

A brief historical survey

Christianity in China over its long history has been interpreted according to different cultural schemes. During the Tang dynasty (seventh to ninth centuries), the
Christian message was introduced to China by missionary monks from the Eastern (Syrian) church. It tended to
be expressed through categories and terms derived from
Buddhism and Daoism.

During the Yuan dynasty (twelfth and thirteenth centuries), Franciscan friars coming from Europe met the
Mongols, then ruling China, and achieved some success
in adapting to the foreign dynasty. However the friars left
no trace on the Chinese population after the advent of the
nationalistic Ming rulers in 1368.

During the period of late Ming and early Qing (sixteenth to eighteenth centuries), Jesuit missionaries and
Christian scholars tried to integrate Christianity with
Confucian imperial ideology, emphasising the ethical
aspect of Christian doctrine. But the majority of the literati, satisfied with the strong ethical basis of Confucian
thought, saw no need for Christian teaching. As a consequence Christianity, especially after the disastrous out-

come of the controversy over ancestor rites, did not find a significant place in Chinese thought.

In the second half of the nineteenth century, Christianity (this time in its various streams of Catholic, Protestant and Orthodox denominations) regained a chance for expansion in China. However, because of the political implications of its presence, Christianity was accused by a number of Chinese intellectuals and political leaders of being a religion not only foreign to Chinese culture, but also compromised by western imperialist interests. Such a harsh condemnation, which largely overlooked the positive contribution by Christian churches to the development of social and educational services in China, was the ideological justification of communist repression during the Maoist decades (1949–1976).

The victimisation of the intellectuals

Besides the believers, intellectuals were also violently targeted during the Maoist political campaigns, especially during the Cultural Revolution. Intellectuals and students since the May Fourth Movement (1919) had assumed a leading role in the process of modernisation of the nation. In the late 1970s some intellectuals and artists expressed the frustration and pain caused by the humiliation and persecution they had suffered as victims of the Cultural Revolution. Such experiences of spiritual and human misery gave birth to a new interpretive model that has been called 'the literature of the wounded'. Against such a background, the academic world and Christianity began a new encounter where Christian thought offered a profound understanding of the meaning of life and a means of interpreting the existential drama they had gone through.

Numerous intellectuals began to investigate aspects of western thought and religion which had been previously been considered taboo, in order to get to know things that they had previously rejected unexamined. A call for reform swept over China in the '80s, and the famed television series *He Shang*, in June 1988, was a momentous episode in the quest for reform.

At the end of the decade Chinese intellectuals experienced a further blow. The Tiananmen Square massacre (4 June 1989) seemed to proclaim the definitive collapse of Marxism and the historic role of the Communist party, and to emphasise the necessity to search elsewhere for 'national salvation'.[1] After the crackdown that followed, the intellectuals who did not go into exile had to face hard times, injustices and harassment. Some halted writing, translating and publishing. But the existential drama had drawn a number of them close to Christian faith and teaching, generating the phenomena of 'Christianity fever'[2] and of 'cultural Christians', especially amongst Chinese youth.

Li Pingye, a Chinese official and scholar of Christianity who is a member of the United Front organisation of the Communist Party, described the phenomena in the following fashion:

---

1. See below for further comments on this key notion.
2. See *Tripod* no. 83, 1994, an issue devoted to 'Christianity fever'. *Tripod* is Hong Kong based journal on Christianity and China.

They [intellectuals] began a process of self-questioning which extended to the entire history of the Chinese people. They began to doubt the meaning and the value of everything they had been involved in, and they questioned everything they themselves had previously supported and criticized.[3]

In the early 1990s Chinese scholars, such as Liu Peng from the Chinese Academy of Social Sciences, described 'Christianity fever' as a 'mania without precedent in China'.[4] In 1993 Wu Yin, a researcher from the same Academy, acknowledged the existence of a

'Christian cultural phenomenon', a group of scholars who are not Christians but who recognize the value of Christianity and believe that it may play a positive role in helping the formation and development of a pluralist culture in modern China.[5]

In this intellectual climate, from the beginning of the '80s, Chinese translations of many modern and contemporary

---

3. Li Pingye, 'The Attitude of Contemporary Chinese Intellectuals Toward Christianity', in Philip L Wicker and Lois Cole, *Christianity and Modernization: A Chinese Debate* (Hong Kong: Daga Press, 1995), 61.
4. Liu Peng, 'Church and State Relations in China: Characteristics and Trends', in *Tripod*, 88 (1995): 12.
5. Wu Yi, 'The Faith and Life of Christians in Beijing. Interviews and Reflections,' in *China Study Journal*, 8 (1993): 9.

works of theology and studies of Christianity had begun to appear.[6] Influenced by this kind of literature, several scholars, each working within their own discipline (in particular philosophy, history, literary criticism and sociology), explored the Christian response to modern dilemmas. When, in the '90s conditions in the universities improved again, the study of Christianity began to take on a more organised form in twenty or more prestigious universities and research institutes.[7]

These centres for the study of Christianity are mostly affiliated with departments of philosophy, literature or religious studies. Chinese academics have become aware that in many countries, amongst them the United States, religious studies are regularly included amongst the humanities. This has enhanced the status of Christian studies and diminished the discrimination and suspicion they aroused. However, the fact that Christianity is considered a foreign religion, tied up with western interests, still to-

---

6. Amongst the Christian writers translated were Søren Kierkegaard, Dietrich Bonhoeffer, Paul Tillich, Karl Barth, Rudolf Bultmann, Reinhold Niebuhr, Wolfhart Pannenberg, Paul Ricoeur, and Hans Küng.

7. Among the main ones are: Peking University; The People's University (Beijing); Chinese Academy of Social Sciences (Beijing); Nationalities University (Beijing); Foreign Languages University (Beijing); Nanjing University; University of Heilongjiang (Harbin); Nankai University (Tianjin); Shandong University (Jinan); Henan University (Kaifeng); Shaanxi Normal University (Xi'an); Fudan University (Shanghai); Shanghai University; Zhejiang University (Hangzhou); Zhongshan University (Guangzhou); Yunnan University (Kunming).

day makes its study somewhat problematic in the eyes of the authorities.

The voices of the intellectuals interested in Christianity make themselves heard through a significant number of books, periodicals, seminars and conferences. However, along with strict control by the authorities, the progress of Christian studies is hindered by a scarcity of academic resources. In every area there are deficiencies in the knowledge of the languages, modern and classical, needed for an in-depth study of theology and the history of Christianity. However, this difficulty is being overcome through the great enthusiasm of numerous young scholars who have engaged in the study of languages and classical traditions, with the support of international academic institutions.

There is no lack of other encouraging signs. For the first time Christian thought is developing spontaneously, without the influence of western missionaries. The academic world (or rather, part of it) recognises a right of citizenship for Christian thought previously denied it. For centuries, intellectuals—with the exception of the Confucian friends of Matteo Ricci, Xu Guangqi, Li Zhizao, Yang Tingyun and a few others—fiercely contested the very legitimacy of the Christian presence in China. Today, on the other hand, the great majority of students of Christianity seem to have overcome the anti-religious and anti-Christian ideological prejudices that once prevailed, such as treating religion as pre- or anti-scientific[8] and Christianity as a foreign religion supporting the interests of the West in China.[9]

Christian studies have also received stimulus from the revival of religion and especially the growing interest in Christianity amongst the young, particularly university students. It should be noted, however, that Christian churches, still controlled by the regime, have not yet been able to participate actively in the development of Christian studies despite their deep sympathy for their development. Some years ago Ding Guangxun, the Protestant Bishop of Nanjing and the major leader of the Protestants, affirmed that 'Christianity is enjoying today a better receptivity from Chinese intellectuals than at any time since its first arrival in its Nestorian form in 635'.[10]

Who are these intellecuals and what are they saying?

Who are the 'cultural Christians'?

Liu Xiaofeng

Liu Xiaofeng, an intellectual educated in the People's Republic, is considered the 'father' and prototype of cultural Christians. Through his productivity and vivacity of ex-

---

8. The fundamental current official position on religion and its future decline in a scientific age is enunciated in *Document 19* (31 March 1982).
9. This judgment is advanced at least in part in the Chinese government *White Paper on Religious Liberty in China* (October 1997).
10. VKH. Ting, 'Christianity and Chinese Intellectuals: History and the Present', in *Chinese Theological Review*, 11/2 (1997): 71–75.

pression he has played a central role in the debates about Christian studies in China. He seems to have coined the term 'cultural Christian' and to have been the centre of a lively debate about the concept.[11]

Liu studied theology in Switzerland during the 1980s and then directed the Center for Sino-Christian Studies in Hong Kong (Tao Feng Shan in Shatin). Between 1988 and 1989, Liu Xiaofeng wrote a series of ten articles on the theology of the twentieth century for *Du Shu* (*Reading*), the most popular intellectual journal in China.[12] Toward the end of the series Liu mentions the concept of the 'cultural Christian' in the course of a discussion of Simone Weil.

'Cultural Christians', according to Liu, are those scholars who approach Christianity through their studies and personal aspirations. Christianity becomes for them a kind of orientation for their personal and moral life, and for some, for their spiritual life as well, so that the Christian faith becomes something personal to which they adhere conscientiously. This does not mean that they enter the church, either Protestant or Catholic, or seek baptism.

Those who reject the label may do so for various reasons. For some it is simply an abuse of language: one is either Christian or not. Fascinated by the mystical dimension of the faith, or influenced by liberal literature, some might think the church a product of history, an institution that kills the spirit. But there are also other reasons

---

11. For this debate see the collection in Chinese by scholars from Hong Kong, the PRC and Taiwan under the title *Christians: Cultural Phenomenon and Debate*, (Tai Fong Shan: Institute of Sino-Christian Studies, 1997).
12. Published monthly by SDX Joint Publishing, Beijing.

why they remain 'cultural' rather than becoming 'ecclesial' Christians. They might consider the official churches, controlled by the Patriotic Associations and the government (Religious Affairs Bureau), as lacking in authentic religious spirit. And, of course, it is impossible for them to join the underground communities, or the 'house churches', and to continue their academic activities. Some Chinese scholars of Christianity who prefer to avoid being called 'cultural Christians', adopt the neutral title of 'Scholars in Mainland China Studying Christianity'. In this way they steer clear of suspicion from the political authorities, which permit Christian studies only if they remain in the realm of exclusively academic activities.

Nonetheless the term 'cultural Christians' has had remarkable success, and I am using it in this short study because it is still unknown to many, and because I find it a stimulating and apt term to represent a transitional, not-too-clearly delineated, complex and interesting phenomenon.

The Sino-theology of Liu Xiafeng

The program of constructing a Sino-theology, or, more literally, a theology in the Han Language, is one of the most exacting tasks engaged in by Liu Xiaofeng and by the cultural Christians. Sino-theology is not a 'sinisation' (*zhongguohua*) of theology, that is, it is not western theology translated into Chinese. Sino-theology is rather the elaboration of a genuinely Christian theology in Chinese language and thought patterns. When this is achieved, Sino-theology can stand on the same level as theologies in Greek, Latin, French and so on.

According to Liu, rather than concerning itself with being in its transcendental essence, Sino-theology is concerned with being in its specific dimension of time and space. In other words, Sino-theology does not aim at expressing in Christian terms the great Chinese religious and moral traditions that Liu calls systems of national thought: Confucianism, Daoism and Buddhism. This procedure would be similar to the adoption of Platonism and Aristotelianism by western theologians.

The form of theology proposed by Liu privileges the existential experience that is known only in its specific linguistic context. In order to understand and express the encounter with Christ in one's life (the 'Christ event'), Sino-theology adopts the existential-personal-concrete-historical and local dimension of linguistic expression rather than national systems of thought. The act of faith in fact relates to the existential experience of the person rather than to the system of national thought.

What is specifically Chinese in this proposal is the language, the Chinese language: Liu Xiaofeng has elaborated a 'mother-tongue theology' (*muyu shenxue*), that is, a theology that adopts mother language as the tool of expression. The material of theology in a mother tongue is the existential experience and the cultural resources expressed by that language. The auditors of theology in a mother tongue are principally those who speak that language.

Language is here intended not as an external modality of communication, as a tool, but as the specific existential form of expressing one's own reality, according to the theories of Martin Heidegger and Ludwig Wittgenstein.

Language is not an indifferent option; it is the way one brings his/her own self to a conceptual existence. Language is the abode of existence, its form and its boundary. Language is not only the instrument of thought, but it is itself thought.

Sino-Christian theology

Since Liu Xiaofeng interrupted his theological reflections about Sino-theology,[13] there has been a shift of terminology and objectives: today's authors prefer the notion of Sino-Christian theology. Sino-Christian theology is less existentially charged than Liu's Sino-theology, and allows more space for the social and ethical issues faced by the nation.

Professor Sun Shangyang[14] from Beijing University, affirms that Sino-Christian theology aims for Christian thought to gain right of citizenship in the academic, intellectual and cultural world. Professor Sun praises the Jesuits and their late Ming Confucian friends who presented Christian thought as *Tianxue*, Science of Heaven. Although the strategy failed because of the dispute over

---

13. Since 2001, Liu Xiaofeng has taught Political Philosophy at Zhong-shan University, Guangzhou.
14. Professor of Christianity at the University of Beijing, Sun Shang-yang has written a lot about the history of Christianity in China and is interested now in the role that Sino-Christian theology might play in contemporary Chinese thought. For what follows see his 'A Reflection on the Development of Sino-Christian Theology from the Perspective of the History of Chinese Christian Thought', in *Institute of Sino-Christian Studies News*, Hong Kong, July 2007.

Chinese rites and the Emperor's consequent opposition to Christianity, the method remains valid; Professor Sun believes that China will not turn back from its opening to the world and to diversity.

Sino-Christian theology has to engage the social order, and contribute to the national community. According to Professor Sun, Christianity must avoid giving merely personal answers to individual existential crises and should rather provide answers to the ethical crisis of the nation. Christianity (and Christian theology) should maintain a dialectical relationship with society, looking for points of cooperation and at the same time remaining a critical and prophetic voice. According to Professor Sun Christian thought might exert a positive influence in several areas of the social order, such as the ecological emergency. Christianity must also be able to attract new believers, so that it can spread widely among the Chinese people.

The proposals of Liu Xiaofeng and Sun Shangyang on the tasks of Sino-theology and Sino-Christian theology pose fundamental questions. What does it mean to do theology? Who is a theologian? Since the two scholars propose their thoughts outside explicit membership of the church, some suspect that their theology is an academic exercise, but not an ecclesial service.[15] The issue is made ever more complicated by the peculiar situation

---

15. For divergent views on this see *Cultural Christians: Phenomenon and Debate*, edited by Institute of Sino-Christian Studies (Hong Kong: Institute of Sino-Christian Studies, 1996) [in Chinese].

of 'supervised freedom' in China. The author of this study welcomes, however, that theological reflection exceed the boundaries of theological schools and enter into the classrooms of Chinese universities.

Catholic engagement in Sino-theology

The phenomena of cultural Christians and the task of elaborating an inculturated theology and Christian experience are major challenges for the Catholic theological world. I hope that a growing number of theologians in the Chinese church will participate in this endeavour. The number of students of theology is growing—laypersons, sisters and priests pursuing higher academic education in various international institutions. They are certainly in a position to engage in a profitable discussion and collaboration with intellectuals and scholars in China. It would be regrettable if the great Catholic theological tradition and the contemporary Catholic theological contribution were marginalised in Christian studies in mainland China. Catholic institutions of higher education must take up this challenge, since there is space for more people to get involved, especially Chinese teachers of theology.

An inculturated Christianity requires also spiritual and ecclesial experience. Inculturation cannot be achieved through academic and intellectual discourse alone. A number of inculturation experiments may have brought few results because of a lack of deep faith commitment. I also believe that people who have received this charism and prophetic gift can bring about theological innovations. A faith genuinely and genially expressed through cultural means is at once a grace from above and a mission to be accomplished. These are not things that can be decided over a table.

Meanwhile, the continuing work being done in Christian studies in China provides a major resource for the development of Chinese Christian theology. We will now briefly look at some contributors to the debate.

Between Marxism and Christianity: Wang Yilin

In his series of articles that appeared in *Du Shu* Liu Xiaofeng singled out Simon Weil (1909–1944), the French social activist, writer and philosopher of Jewish origin, as the prototype of the cultural Christian. Liu was attracted by the anti-establishment, irregular, and anti-institutional elements of Simone Weil's Christian faith, and her existence as a Christian without baptism and church. A few years ago I had a chance to talk about Simone Weil with Wang Yilin (not his real name), a cultural Christian from Shanghai, and this private conversation may help us understand what the concept entails. Professor Wang said in April 2000, during a conversation at a coffee shop in Shanghai,

> I am translating some of Simone Weil's works, because I find her personal experience fascinating. Her story made up of ideology and faith, struggles and failures, delight, joy and death, touches and speaks to the heart of many intellectuals like me. She had ideals, illusions and suffering like us intellectuals. She

discovered Christianity after passing through Communism and oriental religions. Hers is a Christianity without a church; hers is an incarnated and mystical faith, which seems closer to our pain.

My interlocutor is a teacher of Marxism with a passion for Christianity. His approach is philosophical in character. He has read Thomism and Neo-Thomism; he knows Jacques Maritain, and is translating into Chinese a number of the writings of Simone Weil, a figure that fascinates both of us.

I tell my friend about an episode in Weil's life that has touched me deeply. One evening in Portugal, where she had gone for health reasons, Weil took part in a religious procession in a fishermen's village. The songs of grief and anguish of the poor women, widows and wives of the fishermen on the high seas profoundly touched Simone Weil's sensitive and broken heart. She felt 'Christianity is indeed the religion of the oppressed'. That touches me because this is the exact opposite of Marxism's 'religion is the opium of the people'.

Wang's response to my remark surprised me:

'I would say rather,' he commented, 'that Marxism is the opium of the oppressed, in that it offers them an illusory hope.'

'You are a teacher of Marxism,' I responded, perplexed. 'How can you reconcile these reflections with what you teach?'

'Teaching Marxism is my work. I have to live! Very few want to teach it, but since courses in Marxism are obligatory for the students of all departments, a great number of teachers are needed, and so it is relatively easy to find a teaching post in Marxism. But my personal interest lies in Christian thought'.

Christianity as the 'Spirit' of the West: Li Pingye

Li Pingye, whom I quoted above, is an official of the Communist Party and the United Front, and a student of Christianity who has shown a significant intellectual sympathy for and a remarkable closeness to cultural Christians. Li Pingye describes in her article, almost in anguish, the devastating consequences of China's frenzied modernisation:

> Worship of money, hedonism, extreme individualism, covetousness, corruption, drugs, prostitution, crime ... We have become lone souls, that wander in an endless spiritual void. The future is to be feared: what will become of the Chinese people?

In a society where the market is paramount, a number of intellectuals, marginalised by the logic of the market, find in Christian thought and faith a moral and spiritual way out.

Li Pingye also noted that when the policy of openness began (1978), Chinese intellectuals looked with dismay at the gaps between the material and spiritual progress of western civilisation, and China's cultural and material backwardness. Seized with nationalistic pride, the intellectuals went to the West, both physically and psychologically, to study the reason for the West's success in order to transplant it back to China. They discovered that 'Christianity is at the source of human values and ethical norms'. In a word, the scholars noted how much Christianity had positively influenced every aspect of the western world. They thus realised that to understand the West one must know Christianity and how it enabled western civilisation to develop science and technology, the arts, education, democracy and human rights, in a word: modernisation. While the collapse of Marxist ideology and the introduction of the market economy have damaged China's ethical foundations, Li Pingye detects in Christian thought a moral resource for the country.[16]

She is not alone among scholars who seek to introduce into China the cultural foundations that enabled the 'Christian West' to modernise. This is to see Christianity as instrumental in 'national salvation', the historic mission that Chinese intellectuals have embraced ever since the May Fourth Movement.[17] Such a historical reference is highly suggestive since the two pillars of the 1919 movement were science and democracy; however, after 1919, these were increasingly seen as antithetical to Christian-

16. Li Pingye, 'The Attitude of Contemporary Chinese Intellectuals Toward Christianity', in *Christianity and Modernization: A Chinese Debate*, edited by P Wickeri and L Cole (Hong Kong: DAGA Press, 1995), 59–77.

17. The May Fourth Movement of 1919 was a crucial moment in Chinese history. It began as a student protest against the provisions of the Treaty of Versailles but became a general movement to redress a century of humiliation by replacing Confucian values with western models.

ity. The cultural Christians, on the contrary, see them as underpinned by Christian values.

A new moral foundation: Yang Huilin[18]

The quest for a new moral foundation described by Li Pingye is continued by another cultural Christian, Yang Huilin, director of the Institute for the Study of Christian Culture of Renmin University in Beijing.

The 'literature of the wounded' which appeared in the early 1980s described the frustration and pain experienced by Chinese intellectuals, a category especially victimised during the Cultural Revolution, a national tragedy now referred to as 'The Ten Disastrous Years'.

Yang Huilin reflects upon the moral disaster and failure of the Cultural Revolution, arguing that it was for Chinese intellectuals what the Shoah (or Holocaust) was for European believers and theologians. How could such tragedies occur? How could the Shoah happen in Europe, a culture imbued with two thousand years of Christianity? How could the Cultural Revolution happen in the

---

18. Yang Huilin, Professor of Chinese Literature, founded the Institute of Christian Culture Studies at Chinese People's University in Beijing in 1995. Since 1998 this institute has published a periodical *Christian Culture Study Journal*, which appears twice a year. Among Yang's publications (in Chinese) are: *Sin and Salvation: A Theory of the Spirit of Christian Culture*, (Beijing: Dongfang, 1995) and *Asking for God: A Debate between Faith and Reason* (Beijing: Beijing Education Publishing House, 1999). For this section, I refer to my numerous conversations with Professor Yang Huilin; to his book *Asking for God*; and to an article by Leo Leeb, 'Yang Huilin and his View of Christian Culture,' in *Inter-religio* 38 (2000): 58–65.

five thousand year old Chinese civilisation, imbued with Confucian humanism?

The root of contemporary interest in Christian thought in China might be precisely here. According to Yang Hui-lin, the tragedy of the Cultural Revolution that he himself experienced, pinpointed the need for a new ethical order, and for a new relation between conscience and authority. Yang affirms that the greatest contribution that Christianity can offer to China today is 'an absolute morality'. The absoluteness of the moral good, radically opposed to evil, is guaranteed only by the existence of a transcendent God, and the total 'otherness' of God in respect to human events. In the Chinese tradition, on the other hand, according to Yang, the human and the divine, politics and religion, action and norms, have always been profoundly intermingled, so that moral judgment could easily be distorted and controlled by secular interests. Confronted with the ideological ends of Marxism and the crisis of classical thought, only Christianity can offer, according to Yang, the solid ethical foundation that modern China desperately needs.

As a consequence of all this, Yang Huilin stresses the 'difference', the 'otherness', and the 'newness' of Christianity in respect to Chinese thought. In a counter-current way, Yang is critical of Christianity's attempts at inculturation, including those of Matteo Ricci. He fears that in some way inculturation might lessen the distinctiveness of Christianity; Yang wants Christian thought to safeguard and to promote its 'difference'.

Professor Yang promotes Christian studies in a systematic way in his university where in 1995 he founded the Institute for the Study of Christian Culture. Since 1998 Yang has been publishing an important semi-annual periodical entitled *Christian Culture Study Journal*, in which Chinese and international authors publish numerous, in-depth Christian studies. At the same university, the Chinese government in 2000 established the National Centre for Research in Religious Sciences, offering financial resources and more academic autonomy. The section devoted to Christian studies is guided by the same professor Yang.

The humanism and universality of Christianity: He Guanghu[19]

He Guanghu, one of the most respected scholars of Christianity from Mainland China, is also alarmed at the moral collapse in the country, and sees in Christianity 'a hope for

---

19. He Guanghu served as research fellow at the Institute of World Religions of the Chinese Academy of Social Sciences. He has gained international appreciation for his studies on Christianity. His studies include: *With the Heart, Without Problems* (Beijing: Sanlian Publishing House, 1997) (in Chinese); 'Religious Studies and Their Connection with Political and Social Circumstances'; 'Some Causes and Features of the "Christian Upsurge" Among Chinese Intellectuals'; 'A Religious Spirit: The Hope for Transnationalism in China Today', all published in *Christian Theology and Intellectuals in China* (University of Aarhus: Centre for Multireligious Studies, 2003). For this section I refer to the Professor's writings, to my conversations with him, and to Matteo Nicolini-Zani, *Gli studi cristiani accademici e il fenomeno dei 'cristiani culturali': una finestra aperta sul cristianesimo nel contesto della cultura cinese odierna*, Venezia, 1999, 178–182 (unpublished dissertation that the Nicolini-Zani has kindly shared with me).

a better China'. He is a former researcher at the Academy of Social Sciences in Beijing and now active in religious studies at the People's University of China in Beijing. He Guanghu thinks that the ethical principles of Christianity cannot be separated from their spiritual source and cannot be reduced to an instrument of modernisation. Christianity is a universal religion that brings a spiritual message that speaks to the heart of people and touches their humanity. He Guanghu, who also experienced the moral crisis and suffering of the Chinese people, does not let himself fall into pessimism. He continues to believe in the human spirit, and maintains that modernisation must, above all, be a work of humanisation, reaching to the centre of the heart — that is, it involves human persons and their values, including spiritual ones.

> I believe that the heart suffices to minimize many problems. If there were a little more altruism in the world, a little more patience, generosity, love and trust, if there were a little more sense of communion, responsibility, tolerance, sentiment, justice and benevolence, how many problems would be resolved.[20]

He Guanghu maintains that Christianity cannot be reduced to a 'spirit of Western civilisation'; it is rather a religion with a strong humanistic and universal character. As such, Christianity has the innate capacity for dialogue

---

20. He Guangho, *With the Heart: Without Problems*, preface.

with all cultures, and can be considered in continuity with the best of China's cultural and religious traditions.

Rather than stressing the 'otherness' of Christianity, as Yang Huilin does, He Guanghu advocates the inculturation of Christianity in China and its dialogue with the Chinese thought. He considers the continuity between these two traditions as possible, useful, and also necessary. In a vision, perhaps even too optimistic, that recalls the thought of the great Christian thinker John Wu Jingxiong,[21] He Guanghu sees in Christianity the supreme synthesis of Chinese wisdom:

> When Confucianism's adoration of heaven is separated from the idolatry and the cult of fortune telling; when Buddhism's aspiration for perfection is separated from the flight from and contempt for the world; when Taoism's respect for life is separated from the practice of superstition, then we come very close to pure Christianity.[22]

---

21. John Wu Jingxiong (1899–1986) attempted to develop a synthesis between Christian humanism and that of Confucius, between Christian spirituality and Daoist 'mysticism'. In his small masterpiece, *The Science of Love: A Study in the Teachings of Thérèse of Lisieux* (Hong Kong: Catholic Truth Society, 1941) John Wu, with deep spiritual emotion, interprets the experience and writings of St Therese of Lisieux in terms of Confucian humanism and Daoist spirituality. His stimulating thought can also be found in the collection of his studies, *Beyond East and West* (London: Sheed & Ward, 1951).

22. He Guanghu, *With the Heart: Without Problems*, 363.

He Guanghu is far from being the only Chinese scholar to call for a new humanism in China with Christian foundations. For reasons of space we cannot consider here the contribution of other important students of Christianity such as Zuo Xinping,[23] Gao Shining,[24] You Xilin,[25] Chen Cunfu,[26] Zhang Qingxiong.[27] These scholars, like the others discussed previously, have overcome the ideological prejudice against Christianity. It is to be hoped that they will continue to influence the governing authorities and society in general towards a new era of Chinese humanism. From many directions there are

---

23. Zhuo Xinping is the most illustrious scholar of Christianity in China. He is director of the Institute of World Religions of the Chinese Academy of Social Sciences in Beijing and author of dozens of publications in which he discusses the themes of philosophy of religion in China and the West, the relationship of religion to culture and the significance of Christianity for Chinese culture and society.

24. Professor in the Chinese Academy of Social Sciences, Gao Shining has translated into Chinese numerous classics of Western theology. She is the author of many studies, especially on the subject of Marxism and Christianity and new religions.

25. You Xilin is Director of the Centre for the Study of Christian Culture at the Normal University of Shaanxi (Xi'an). Although little known, he is a serious contributor to the discussion; he sees in Christianity the spiritual energy that alone can endow the process of modernisation with soul.

26. The pioneer of Christian Studies in China, Chen Cunfu established and directs the Centre for Research in Christianity of the University of Zhejiang. Founded in 1991, it was the first centre for Christian Studies within a Chinese university. Since 1995 Professot Chen has published in Hangzhou *Religion and Culture*, a series on Christian themes by Chinese and other authors.

27. Professor Zhang Qingxiong, whose research is in phenomenology and Christian theology, is a graduate of the University of Freiburg.

calls for a humanisation of the tumultuous transition to modernity underway in China. Christian studies may serve to integrate the 'new morality' sought by intellectuals with Christian thought founded on the spiritual message of the gospel. Once they have overcome the risk of an instrumental approach to Christianity, the reflection of cultural Christians may offer a valuable contribution not only to the advancement of the Chinese nation, but of the Christian thought in the world as a whole.

Chapter Two

Spirited Conversations

Claudia Devaux

Claudia Devaux

'Li Madou? We know him from our math books!' That
was the enthusiastic response of my Chinese postgradu-
ate students when I brought up the name of seventeenth-
century Jesuit Matteo Ricci, remembered in China for his
contributions to science and remembered in contemporary
Christian circles for his passionate embrace of the Chinese
culture, a model of what we refer to now as inculturation.
We Westerners tend to forget that it was Matteo Ricci who
translated the works of Confucius into Latin and thereby
contributed indirectly to the development of Enlightenment thinking, whereas the Chinese do not forget that he
translated Euclid into their language. Ingrained in Ricci
and, before him, in Francis Xavier, the first Jesuit missionary, was a zeal for conversation perfected by Ignatius of

Loyola, the founder of the Society of Jesus and the author
of the Spiritual Exercises.

I had brought up the name Li Madou to explain to my
students that I had been absent for a few days in order to
attend a conference in Beijing on the history of the Jesuits
in China. Having pored over books on the Communist
takeover (known in China as the 'Liberation') and the
Cultural Revolution as I worked with a twentieth-century
Chinese Jesuit on his memories of arrest and imprisonment, I had not expected the students to be aware of Ricci,
much less appreciative of him. But they were enthusiastic, seemingly pleased that they and I had, in a sense, this
aspect of a shared heritage. In fact, one group of students
chose as the topic for their research paper the contributions of the Jesuits to science in China.

That semester I had one hundred first-year graduate students intent on learning to write a research paper
in English. At my instruction they worked with class-
mates—fellow scholars—whom they trusted and with
whom they would enjoy having tea. They formed their
own teams to do research on a topic of their choice and
submit a well-documented and well-formatted academic
paper that they would defend in a face-to-face meeting
with me. The students were required to craft a research
question, review the literature on the topic, and then to
engage in fieldwork involving conversations with willing
participants. The conversations in Chinese were record-
ed, transcribed as triplets of lines—the first line in pinyin,
the second a literal English translation of the first, and the
third a line of polished English. The students would then
analyse the text and search for emerging themes. While

the paper on the contributions of the Jesuits had the potential for following this model, I was disappointed that the students had designed a synthesising report rather than a participatory research project. At the same time, however, I was intrigued by this team's choice of topic and agreed that they could pursue it. What remains in my mind is their conclusion that in spite of Li Madou's significant contributions, including teaching his Chinese contemporaries to use instruments invented two hundred years before by their ancestors but for which no written instructions had been provided, his motivation was nevertheless to convert people to his religion.

How did my students, and others whom I encountered in China, feel about religion? Certainly it was not a topic that I could bring up with them directly, for my agreement with the government of the People's Republic of China included a stipulation against proselytising, and I did not want even to be perceived as trying to convert people to my religion. Having taken part in an orientation program organised in Hong Kong by the Maryknoll Fathers, I was keenly aware that I would be watched and even tested. The 'test' came early in the semester when two second-year graduate students—not my own students—showed up during office hours in my quarters at the residence for foreign teachers. One came with a problem: he was, he said, at a crossroads in his life and concerned about his 'immortal soul'—and the other, I suspected, was there to witness the interview. The term 'immortal soul' is not in frequent use today; it rings of another era in ecclesial history, and hearing the student pronounce these words raised a red flag in my mind. I asked the student to tell me something about himself. He was not a young man; he was already forty years old, and he had a daughter. Perhaps he was on the verge of a mid-life crisis, but it seemed strange that he would seek out a foreign teacher for advice. I expected visits about thesis topics or debate preparation. Still, we talked about his daughter. This went on for two meetings, each time with the companion present, as the student indicated he was searching for holiness. He spoke of his love for his daughter and eventually acknowledged that love was a holy feeling. After the second meeting, I saw neither the student nor his companion again, but since the dean asked me to consider staying on past the one year of my contract, I assumed that a report had been made and that I had passed the 'test'.

In the first or second week of the fall semester, in order to gauge their writing proficiency, I asked the students to write an essay about a personal experience. Some of the essays were absolutely delightful, and others were agonising. There were at least three essays on women's rights, and I learned that Chairman Mao had proclaimed that 'women hold up half the sky'. A male student wrote about an unhappy incident that was 'not a blessing in disguise'. A few students told of the sacrifices made by their parents so that they might get an education. One young woman described being in the military, voicing her deep commitment to her country and to discipline. Another young woman wrote about having attended a Christian youth camp. She looked upon the organisers in a condescending manner, commenting on the naïveté of their belief that the world was created in six days. I made a point of noting on her paper that not all Christians interpreted the Bible literally.

Two young men wrote bitterly about specific incidents of social injustice, and they explicitly asked for my comments on the issues. It was a dilemma for me. First, I wanted to return their papers immediately, but I would not see them in class, since I was about to go away for the conference in Beijing. Second, I had to be careful not to 'get involved' in internal affairs. Third, besides being careful for myself, I did not want the students to be criticised if an administrator or classmate read their papers and interpreted their essays as inappropriately raising internal issues with a foreign teacher; therefore I could not simply leave the papers in the office for students to collect. And so I bought one hundred large format envelopes and inserted one essay into each. After addressing and sealing the envelopes, I went to the graduate student dormitory and distributed them room by room; there were three students to each room. My comments on the papers regarding the social justice issues were something to the effect of its always being painful to observe or hear about something that we find unjust. But the two students did not let up. Another paper, perhaps not even an assignment, reached me on a similar topic. This time I was more direct, writing on the papers and speaking individually to the authors that, as a foreign teacher, I was not permitted to comment on these issues. I thought the students understood. However, at the end of the school year, when they filled out an evaluation on my teaching, one made a point of letting me see that he gave me a low mark on 'caring about students' whereas every other student gave

me very high marks. To this day, I regret the missed opportunity to engage in a meaningful conversation about
social justice with this young man.

Fortunately there were many fruitful conversations.
One group of students did research on modern Chinese
women and Buddhism. From the transcription of conversations with one of their participants, they saw that while
she might have consulted a priest looking for a 'magic'
solution to her problems, he guided her to search within
herself. The 'ah ha' moment that happened as the students
were discussing their work came about when they real-
ized that the experience of the woman was not so much
about superstition as it was about gaining insight, about
Buddha saying, 'I am awake'. It seemed that the students
were relieved to find that spirituality is not necessarily
the antithesis to reason.

Not concerned about how Buddhism was perceived
was a student from the neighbouring law school who
visited me regularly, even bringing flowers on Moth-
ers' Day. On one occasion he arrived with a wide smile,
anxious to let me know that he had been invited to join
the Party. We celebrated by having dinner at a campus
restaurant. A few days later, he asked me to accompany
him and his friend to a temple where we lit incense and
he prayed in thanksgiving. He was not aware that being
a Party member precludes religious affiliation, and I did
not mention it. Perhaps in contemporary China, a land of
puzzles and paradoxes, visiting a temple is not the same
as religious affiliation. One pleasant young woman who
visited regularly confided that she was a Christian. I did
not ask her about her affiliation but had the impression

that she attended a house church. We never talked specifically about religion again although we were very close. Another woman voiced her concern when some of the foreign teachers chose fabric with embroidered dragons to have clothes made for their relatives; she explained that her mother was a Christian who viewed the dragons as demonic. I refrained from trying to explain to her that one twentieth-century Jesuit from California, Father Francis Rouleau, was known in China as 'Celestial Dragon'. While she may have been confused by our not taking dragons for evil, she observed, however, that we took stewardship of the earth very seriously, picking up papers as we walked across campus and tossing them into trash bins. Soon she was collecting litter along her path.

Christian teachers were allowed to take two days off at Christmas. I chose Christmas Eve and Christmas Day, and others chose Christmas Day and Boxing Day. Some of my students asked to attend Midnight Mass with me, and I told them that although I could not have them go to the church with me, I would be happy to meet them there. The streets were extremely crowded on Christmas Eve. In general, there were no holidays from work or school at Christmas, and yet it was a time of joyful dancing, singing, and merrymaking in the streets. Young people explained to me that since Christmas was not a Chinese holiday and therefore not a family event, it was the one occasion during the year when they could simply have fun with their peers. Pushing our way through throngs of people, my colleagues and I reached the gated entrance to a park. We would have to walk through the park to get to the church, but the gates were locked and people stood in long lines to purchase entry tickets and be admitted one by one. I protested to a guard who let us enter without tickets ahead of the others. My students were in another noisy crowd gathered outside the illuminated church. We squeezed inside and made our way to the tribunal. At first I tried to explain what was going on during the Mass, but that was distracting and it seemed best just to let their senses take in the sights and sounds. Afterwards, a taxi was not able to get us back to campus, so thick were the crowds and so congested the streets. And so we went on foot, a little concerned that the guard might not admit the students to the dorm after curfew. I accompanied them to the dorm, and the guard kindly opened the gate for them.

Also attending the Mass on Christmas Eve was a little girl whom I had met in the tribunal of the church one October Sunday. After that Sunday Eucharist, she followed my colleagues and me down the path toward the park, pointing to one of the teachers and asking in English, 'Who is he?' I replied that he was a friend, and she responded, 'Jolly good!' I gave her my card, and soon I started receiving phone calls from someone with a wee little voice. She would speak to me in Chinese and, without understanding, I would listen for a couple of minutes, and then I would tell her that I had enjoyed the conversation. We would say 'good bye' until the next time. I am not sure if her parents were Catholic or even Christian. It was unusual to see children at Mass except as musicians at Christmas or Easter. That Christmas Eve, the little girl had insisted that her mother bring her to Mass, but the mother was anxious to get the child home to bed, for the next day was a school day.

The university campus was aglow with fairy lights in the trees that graced the entrance. The festive sparkle would continue every night until after Chinese New Year. Just before Christmas, in an effort to share something of the season with my classes, I read to them O Henry's 'The Gift of the Magi' only to learn that they were quite familiar with the story. On Christmas Day itself, we foreign teachers had our own repast, each of us having volunteered to provide something. We had debated about what to do for our holiday meal, whether to go to the Marriott or the Holiday Inn for a 'traditional' dinner, but the consensus was to spend Christmas 'at home' rather than in a restaurant. Our little group represented many countries including Australia, England, Germany, Japan, the Netherlands, Russia, and the United States. We exchanged presents, sang carols, and generally enjoyed the holiday. But I had to hurry off because my dean and the university president emeritus had thoughtfully invited me to dinner in one of the private faculty dining rooms so that I would not miss celebrating Christmas.

Throughout the year, I ended each class session with some kind of brief story which I also posted on my website as the students seemed interested in having a copy. Most of the time the stories were inspirational pieces attributed to the likes of Mother Teresa ('The good that you do today will be forgotten tomorrow. Do good anyway') and Anthony De Mello ('Waking up is difficult . . .') and Chinese folklore. These stories provided fodder for our conversations. We could compare the action-oriented Golden Rule of the West about doing unto others as you would have them do unto you to the more passive Silver

Rule of the East, attributed to Confucius, about not doing to others what you would not want done to yourself.
Could it be that the West tended to get involved in other
people's affairs because of the Golden Rule whereas the
Easterners placed a high value on minding one's own
business? Or, on another note, what about Bó Lè Shí Mǎ
who, in treating a horse that others saw as tired and slug-
gish as a sleek and gracious steed, actually encouraged
him to behave as he was treated? I felt honoured when the
students identified me as Bó Lè Shí Mǎ because I recog-
nised their potential.

I did not encounter many young adults at Mass on
Sundays though the church was always packed. The
congregation was largely made up of elderly people,
some in tattered Mao jackets, who would stand in line
for confession before Mass and then leave some kind of
place-holder in the line, perhaps an umbrella, where they
would return when confessions resumed after Mass and
the Benediction. Upon entering the church before Mass, I
would hear the collective murmur of voices reciting the
rosary; a few of the voices continued during the liturgy.
The choir members and the energetic organist, whom we
joined in the tribunal and with whom we enjoyed warm
exchanges at the sign of peace, were in their thirties and
forties. Occasionally from our perch in the tribunal, we
foreign teachers observed altercations between elderly
parishioners, once even requiring the intervention of the
celebrant.

The priest, Father Liu, a relatively young man, had
responsibility for ten thousand parishioners. Lay people
served as lectors, and among the eucharistic ministers

was a young sister. It turned out that Sister Theresa was a student who lived in a dormitory near me. We talked about serving as ministers, and I seized the opportunity to suggest that she hold the host in front of the communicant, making eye contact, rather than simply placing the bread of life on the tongue or in the hand. She immediately adopted this practice, and so did Father Liu. One day she and I encountered a beggar in the street. She questioned me about offering money to him, and I volunteered that since it would not be possible to help all the beggars, much less to know if they were poor or engaged in some kind of racket, I found it preferable to provide charity in a systematic way. I was given to understand that Father Liu had a program to respond to the needs of the poor, and some of us made contributions of money and clothing.

One day Sister Theresa took me to visit an old folks' home which had once been a nursing school run by a French religious order. The property, which included a large chapel, was being restored for religious use and would house not only the elderly but also a group of young Chinese sisters. I met several senior residents, some wearing crosses, who warmly embraced me as I wondered about the weight of the crosses they bore during the Cultural Revolution, for surely they had suffered for their faith. Happily, life was better for them now; during this visit, they were radiant with joy.

Back on campus, it was the 'office hour' of an Australian teaching couple, Noreen and Bryan Hogan. What was really going on was not a meeting about grammar or syntax or literature. It was the weekly songfest ('I See the

Moon') where the young people were laughing and enjoying slices of watermelon. Students were talking about dreams and values, about their families and their future, about striving to do their best in their studies, and about caring for others. These 'office hours' were very much like meetings of Christian youth groups in the West. Matteo Ricci and other Jesuit missionaries had seen heaven at work in the Chinese culture; they opened the door for ongoing conversations that were sadly slammed shut when the Church condemned the Chinese rites in 1742. The door re-opened a little when, in 1939, that condemnation was lifted but only to be closed again following the 'Liberation' of 1949. The fact that not only does Ricci's name appear respectfully today on the pages of Chinese textbooks but that his grave is reverently tended on the premises of the Beijing Administrative College, where Party members are educated, gives us hope that Ignatian-like conversations are welcome in the Celestial Kingdom. May continuing conversations help visiting teachers and others recognise, like Bó Lè Shí Mǎ, the heaven sent goodness and sincerity of our Chinese interlocutors who have much to offer our global society.

Chapter Three

Belief in China on the Eighth Day

Roderick O'Brien

Roderick O'Brien

The Olympic Games in Beijing had a traditional commencement: the opening ceremony was held on the eighth day of the eighth month in the year 2008, beginning at eight minutes past eight pm. In Chinese tradition the number eight is a lucky number. The sound of the number eight is *ba*, which rhymes with *fa* meaning to develop or grow. *Fa* is used especially in the context of 'grow rich'. Perhaps the Beijingers are not ungrateful that they were not awarded the 2004 Olympics (which went to Athens). The number four is particularly unlucky (the sound rhymes with 'death'), and it would have been very difficult to sell tickets for an opening ceremony on, say, the fourth of April, 2004.

Of course, according to Marxism, numerology and other such traditions are meaningless superstitions. For many years, Marxism claimed a superior standpoint, representing itself as modern, scientific, and infallible. So what has happened in mainland China that all kinds of religion and superstition have returned? And why is the government itself adopting this kind of numerology in an event as public and as iconic as the Olympic Games?

The answer is to be found in China's recent history. This short essay cannot cover all the aspects of history, but will simply select four examples to open the doors to invite the reader into a further journey of discovery. The reader will find that the changes are being played out, not only in the field of ideas, but in very practical areas such as tourism. Because the author is more familiar with the situation of Catholic believers in China, the examples chosen will reflect this.

The end of belief

Many foreign observers have used terminology such as 'the increasing number of believers' in China. But another very important shift has taken place. This is the shift from belief in Marxism, to unbelief. How it happened will be a matter for debate, but the fact is indisputable.

The particular form which Marxism came to have in China is inextricably linked with the utopian vision of Mao Zedong (MaoTse-tung). Through a series of skilful purges and rectification campaigns, Mao ensured that his version of communism should have no competitors in China. Maoism—or more correctly, Mao Zedong Thought—

became a parallel religion with its own belief structure, scriptures, rites, hagiography, and priesthood. Central to this belief structure was the incredible personality cult of Mao, expressed in millions of items of art and culture.[1] Statues of Mao abounded. Even the elderly could join in the rituals by participating in the simple 'loyalty dance'. This parallel religion had its own formulae for confession, for repentance, and for reconciliation.[2] The creed centred on politics, and was expressed largely in political terms.

Did ordinary people ever believe? And if they did, when did they cease to believe? Clearly, by the end of the Great Proletarian Cultural Revolution, a significant number of Chinese had ceased to believe. This number, and the power that they held, was sufficient to cause a great upheaval in the political landscape. The portraits of Mao were torn from the walls—or at least given a context by sharing the public space with portraits of other leaders. The statues of Mao, once so common, are now difficult to find.

The changes which took place after the collapse of Mao's utopian vision required a new order of belief. The Communist Party of China had already coped with such a major change in belief in 1949, on the success of the revolutionary armies. After 1949, the Party no longer permitted revolution, because any new revolution would be against its own regime. Then, Marxism had to change from being a revolutionary vision, to being a prop of the

1. Gordon Bennet and Ronald Montaperto, *Red Guard: The Political Biography of Dai Hsiao-ai* (New York: Anchor, 1972).
2. Robert Jay Lifton, *Thought Reform and the Psychology of Totalism: A Study of 'Brainwashing' in China* (Harmondsworth: Penguin, 1967).

regime. Now in 1976, another new legitimisation was needed. This was attempted in the adoption of the 1981 Resolution on the History of the Communist Party, which attempted to separate Mao Zedong Thought from Mao Zedong the man.[3] It has not succeeded, and now the legitimacy of the un-elected regime rests on four bases: its possession of the instruments of power; its capacity to deliver economic and social goods; its co-option of nationalist sentiment and its success in preventing the emergence of any viable alternative.

Did people believe in Marxism prior to 1976? Available autobiographies suggest that many did believe, or tried to believe.[4] But because heresy was so dangerous, it is hard to know how many people actually believed, and how many just kept their heads down. Yet some evidence of the power of belief in the Maoist utopia can be gained by the scale of change and disorientation that came about when it collapsed. It is fascinating to realise that the greatest modern shift in belief in China is not the re-emergence of Buddhism or Christianity or the emergence of new beliefs, but the end of belief in Marxism. Surely this is not something that happened overnight, and surely some believers are attempting to re-interpret Marxism in other forms than the Maoist utopia. These forms may command some political respect and adherence, but they no longer command quasi-religious belief.

---

3. Benjamin Ostrov, 'Something of Value: The Religious Response to de-Maoization in China', in *The Social Science Journal*, 42 (2005): 55–70.
4. See, for example, Liang Heng and Judith Shapiro, *Son of the Revolution* (London: Chatto and Windus, 1983).

Marxism, as a symbol, may continue to have a place. Professor Wang Gungwu, speaking in 2002,[5] suggested that Marxism has not lost its importance in China, even though he took the view that 'it is quite clear that communism is meaningless now in China'. Marxism, he says, is still needed for continuity and regime legitimacy. Marxism will also serve as the name for a modern ideology which avoids the dangers of patriotism and nationalism, and of traditional Confucian and other values. Finally, Marxism is universalist and future-oriented, both characteristics needed to draw China beyond the parochial. For Professor Wang, Marxism, along with Morality and regime Maintenance, are the three keys to the continuing emergence of China from its Maoist past.

'Building the religious stage to play the economic opera'

Recently a researcher in Hangzhou examined the extent of religious belief among tertiary students in his city. He drew five conclusions from the data. The fourth conclusion is the unique fascination of religious culture. History, philosophy, literature and art can all inspire religious feelings. Even tourist sites, he observed, now open 'religious natural resources'.[6]

---

5. Wang Gungwu, 'The Emergence of China', Radio Australia Asia Pacific Lecture 5 September 2002. Transcript at <www.abc.net.au/ra/ralectures_pdf/wang_lect_1.pdf>. Accessed 19 April 2004.
6. Wang Kang, 'The Current Situation and Countermeasures of the Religious Question Among Hangzhou's Tertiary Students', in *Contemporary Religions Research*, 1 (2007): 22–31.

In March 2007, I visited the city of Zhaoqing in Guang-
dong province. This attractive riverside city is not far from
Guangzhou (Canton) and is accessible by daily direct bus
even from Hong Kong. It is home to the natural Seven
Stars Crags, and the local government has created a park
to bring domestic and international tourists to the site.
But there are plenty of other places with natural beauty,
and tourism officials have to find new ways to compete.
So Zhaoqing provides us with examples of 'religious natural resources'.

There is a temple complex dedicated to Judge Pao (Bao
Gong), a historical figure who is now deified in popular
religion as the personification of justice in China. He was
stationed in Zhaoqing for part of his career, and had a
reputation for honesty and impartiality which has continued through the centuries. His exploits have inspired
ancient dramas and modern telemovies. Devotees, often
praying for justice (or, more probably, simply for success)
in lawsuits, come from mainland China and abroad. The
temple is traditional in style, but was built in recent times.
The newly instituted annual festival draws devotees not
only from the surrounding areas, but from further afield
and especially from Hong Kong. Moreover, the local government has thoughtfully provided further resources. To
the side of the main temple is a smaller temple or shrine
to the god of literature, Wen Chang. To show that this deified literati never had to toil, and enjoyed great success,
he is usually depicted as pot-bellied. His shrine is particularly popular at examination time, as candidates and their
families come to pray for good results. Even with all the
entrepreneurial opportunities in the new era of socialism,

the examinations are as important now as they have ever been. It helps to have a god on your side.

For the Catholic visitor, there is an extra reason to visit Zhaoqing. Here pioneer Jesuit missionary Matteo Ricci and his colleagues began the cultural and religious inter-change that has contributed so much to the development of the Catholic faith in China. Local officials are alert to any kind of religious natural resources, and offered an at-tractive exhibition celebrating Ricci's life and work. At the time of my visit, the exhibition was located in the Bell and Drum Tower of the old city.

A local friend told me that the Ricci exhibition will not be permanently housed in the Bell and Drum Tower. An old building is being renovated adjacent to the Chongxi Pagoda and the exhibition will be moved to that build-ing when it is ready. This is appropriate, because Ricci's house was also adjacent to the Pagoda, although it has long been demolished.

Zhaoqing can simply serve as one example of a na-tion-wide trend to opening or re-opening religious sites.[7] Sometimes, there is no traditional resource to be tapped, and the same result is achieved by creating a religious site where none existed before. Any enterprising local government can 'build the religious stage to sing the eco-nomic opera'. A temple, a shrine, even a church will serve the purpose. But at the same time, these also serve as ad-vertisements for the enduring power of religion, and as advertisements for the possibility of religious belief.

---

7. Sergio Ticozzi, 'Popular Religion in China Today', in *Tripod,* 15/85 (January-February 1995): 26.

Religious morals

When the utopian project of Mao Zedong finally collapsed, one of the observable consequences was that the
morality it propounded also collapsed. In 1981, only a few
years after the Cultural Revolution, a teacher of politics in
a secondary school reported a conversation he overheard:
'Do you like the class on politics?' 'No, it is all cheating.'
This teacher reported further, 'When I talk about the su-
periority of socialism, they laugh, and when I speak about
the rotten character of capitalism they laugh at me.' Others are less cynical but more pessimistic, saying, 'The
years have passed, yet we get nowhere. We do not own
a thing in the world. Reality is too cruel to us. We do not
find it appealing at all. We see through its vanity. We will
not give a damn about anything.'[8]

Philosophers struggled to find an explanation for
this. Ci Jiwei, now out of the mainland and teaching in
Hong Kong, described it as a journey from utopianism,
to nihilism, and then to hedonism.[9] China's people can
observe—and some can participate in—great economic
achievements. But at the same time, China's people can
observe—and many of them participate in—a great shift
in morality. Some writers use phrases like 'moral landslide'. Shanghai is visibly the leader in the economic
achievements. But one Shanghai academic writes:

---

8. The quoted section is from Edmund Tang, *Youth of the Cultural
   Revolution: Social Problems in Post-Revolutionary China* (Brussels: Pro
   Mundi Vita, 1983), 19. Tang cites *Beijing Review* (23 February 1981):
   22.
9. Ci Jiwei, *Dialectic of the Chinese Revolution: From Utopianism to Hedonism* (Standford: Stanford University Press, 1994).

[P]eople can obviously feel the contradiction between economic development and the moral 'landslide'. Today, while we are building a harmonious society, this feeling has become especially obvious. Compared with the ethical standard in the 1950s–1960s and the fine traditions of China which was established several thousand years ago, people nowadays, who have seen a relatively greater moral loss during the period of social transformation, have begun to cry in fear of a 'moral landslide', and even believe that China is now marching towards 'moral breakdown'.[10]

For nearly three decades, the Party authorities have tried to fill the vacancy caused by the collapse of utopian Maoist morality. They offer a new form of socialist morality, under the heading of 'building a socialist civilisation'. A myriad of programmes, from simple slogans through to complex academic discussions, seek to promote this morality among the Chinese people.[11] But the obvious lack of success means that the authorities have also sought to co-opt both the traditions of Confucian morality, and the moral teaching offered by China's various religions.

While Catholic and Protestant Christians may not have

---

10. Chen Xinhan, 'The Moral "Landslide" of China during the Period of Social Transformation', in *Chinese Cross Currents*, 5/1 (January 2008): 124.
11. Xia Weidong, *Outline History of the Construction of Ideological Morality by the Chinese Communist Party* (Jinan: Shandong People's Publishing House, 2006).

roots as deep in Chinese society as Confucianism or even Buddhism, Christians have one advantage: Christianity is perceived as 'modern'. In learning about technological developments, thinking Chinese can see that these developments cannot be divorced from the societies which created them. And, to the Chinese, those societies are clearly religious. As Chinese face modern moral issues, such as bioethical or environmental moral issues, they find that religious believers abroad have already made a considerable contribution to the debates on these issues. Moreover, Christians have some credibility because of their participation in social welfare activities.

This has created a 'window of opportunity' for believers. I have observed this more closely among China's Catholics, and my examples will be chosen from their experiences. However, there are parallels in other religious traditions. When Catholics seek to make a contribution to ethics in China, they move out from a purely Catholic environment to a public environment where there are other—possibly competing—contributors. One of the paths chosen by Catholics in the field of ethics is to dialogue with the authorities. Thus, in February 2005, Fr John Baptist Zhang of the Faith Institute for Cultural Studies (at Hebei Faith Press) organised a conference across religious boundaries, to give participants an opportunity to share ethical beliefs.[12] Besides religious-based leaders, there

---

12. Faith Reporter: 'A Conference on Religion and Ethics' (25--7 February 2005, Shijiazhuang) at <www.chinacatholic.org/English/news/2005530151829.html>. Accessed 15 January 2008. See also <www.chinacathollic.org/fics/xfhg4/news1.htm>. Accessed 20 January 2008.

were about forty Chinese scholars present, as well as officials from the government's Religious Affairs Bureau and the Party's United Front Work Department (which includes responsibility for Party work with believers). In December 2005, Fr Peter Zhao of the Beijing Catholicism and Culture Research Centre organised a conference on China and Catholic Social Teaching.[13] In both of these conferences, some of the emphasis fell on the practical social work activities of the Catholic Church. Catholics in China have a small but growing institutional involvement in welfare works,[14] and this fits with the government's cautious policy of outsourcing welfare to non-government organisations, and of seeking non-government funding.[15] Catholics have responded locally and across the country to the devastating Wenchuan earthquake,[16] and can be expected to further support charitable works in China.

Recognising that many people are seeking a viable moral path, Catholics are including ethical issues in their evangelisation processes. In Ningbo, not far from

---

13. Fides-Mancini, 'Cina: Seminario Sulla Dottrina Sociale Della Chiesa', 10.11.2005 18.34.26
14. Roderick O'Brien, 'Beifang Jinde: Catholic Social Service Centre', in *Tripod*, 20/118 (2000): 57–64.
15. The government seeks religious funding for its 'hope' programme for schools in remote areas, for relief works, and for support of national minorities. See Shanghai Ethnic and Religious Affairs Administration, *Brief Introduction about Religions in Shanghai*, [nd], 8, 24, and 30. The 'three-self' programme set for China's believers by the Party has been set aside to allow religious believers to solicit funds from abroad for approved projects.
16. Union of Catholic Asian News, 'Catholics Rally across China to Help Quake Victims', in *Sunday Examiner*, (25 May 2008): 3.

Shanghai, one parish has been offering a 'Faith Salon' for non-Christians. The topics under discussion at the salon include conscience and ethics. The Salon has been successful in attracting participants to the parish's programme to prepare people for baptism, and this model is being followed in other parishes.[17]

A modernising China needs a modern ethic. And at least some Chinese perceive Christian ethics as offering viable answers to China's needs. 'Christianity,' said one Chinese scholar, 'has become one of the well-alive propositions for the construction of ethical communities as needed by modernising China'.[18]

Shrines and pilgrimages

China has many points of pilgrimage. A devotee can climb the Buddhist peaks, or the Daoist peaks, or cross the waters to Putuoshan and find the shrine of Guanyin. And for Catholics, the principal points of pilgrimage (besides famous tombs) have been Marian shrines.[19] These are scattered around the country, including the shrine at Sheshan on the outskirts of Shanghai, Jianshan in Shan-

---

17. Beifang Gucheng, 'Spread the Good News in Ningbo'at <www. china.catholic.org/English/news/2006417155915.htm>. Accessed 16 January 2008.
18. You Xilin, 'Christianity's Dual Meaning in the Modernisation of China: In Commemoration of the 450th anniversary of the Death of St Francis Xavier', in *Chinese Cross Currents*, 1/1 (January 2004): 34.
19. Jean Charbonnier, *Guide to the Catholic Church in China 2004* (Singapore: China Catholic Communication, 2004).

dong, Donglu in Hebei, and Fuzhou in Fujian.[20] The almost century-old Annunciation Seminary at Pengzhou in Sichuan, itself a centre for local pilgrimage, collapsed during the recent earthquake.

Recently a scholar in the USA, Yang Fenggang, sought to analyse religion in China by establishing three categories: red, black, and grey markets. The 'red market' is that sector of religion permitted (and heavily controlled) by the government. When the controls are tightest, and the needs of believers are not met, argues this author, they turn to the 'black market' of officially banned religions. But the author also suggests that there is a 'gray market' of religions with ambiguous legal status, and perhaps ambiguous religious status.[21] This distinction is helpful, especially for understanding the situation of formal religions which are not on the list of five[22] approved by the government, such as the Orthodox Church, and for understanding the situation of a variety of traditional popular practices such as *qigong* which are related to Daoism.[23] Catholicism operates in all three 'markets', and the Marian pilgrimages as a form of popular devotion may be seen as 'gray'. The same pilgrimage day (in many places the

---

20. Anon, 'Images of Our Lady of China', in *China Bridge*, May 2007 at <www.hsstudyc.org.hk/en/bridge/bridge_0705.html>. Accessed 13 July 2008.
21. Yang Fenggang, 'The Red, Black, and Gray Markets of Religion in China', in *The Sociological Quarterly*, 47 (2006): 93–122.
22. The officially approved religions are: Buddhism, Daoism, Islam, Catholicism, and Protestantism. Obvious omissions are Chinese popular religions, Confucianism as a religion, and Orthodoxy.
23. John Lagerwey, 'Traditional Religious Practices in China Today', in *Tripod*, 25/85 (January 1995): 6.

feast of Mary Help of Christians on 24 May) attracts both 'red' and 'black' Catholic believers.

Pilgrimages are subject to fluctuating control by the government.[24] A foreign pilgrim visiting Donglu found that he was interrogated by police and removed to the train to Beijing.[25] Since one of the key concerns of the government is to maintain social stability, the waxing and waning of controls often relates to social questions beyond the religious field. In April 2008, the religious authorities sought to keep Marian pilgrimages to a local level.[26] Planned pilgrimages from Hong Kong to Sheshan were called off, and traffic controls were put in place to limit the number of pilgrims. However, the government had also instituted a wide variety of controls, apparently connected to preparations for the Olympic Games, and these may have been the wider stimulus for the controls specifically related to pilgrimages.

One unexpected development at the Sheshan shrine occurred during Mass there on 24 May. In his letter to the Chinese people in June 2007, Pope Benedict XVI had included a 'Prayer to Our Lady of Sheshan' to be recited on the day. Fr Raphael Gao, preaching in Sheshan on 24 May 2008, concluded his homily with a part of the

---

24. UCAN, 'Local Government Gives, Then Withdraws Permission for Catholics to Restore Pilgrimage Site' (4 March 2008) at <www.ucanews.com/2008/03/04/local-government-gives-then-with-draws-permission-for-catholics-to-restor-pilgrimage-site/>. Accessed 13 July 2008.
25. Michael Gunn, 'Perils of a Lone Pilgrim', in *The Tablet,* (14 June 2008): 54–55.
26. Union of Catholic Asian News, 'Authorities Urge People to Keep Marian Pilgrimages Local', in *Sunday Examiner,* (11 May 2008): 3.

Pope's prayer. The congregation responded by continuing to recite the prayer to the end. It was recited again before the final blessing.[27] It seems that the pilgrims had already committed the Pope's prayer to memory.[28] At an approved site ('red' in Yang Fenggang's terminology) the priest uses a passage from the Pope's prayer (definitely 'black') and the people respond.

The eighth day of the eighth month

Which brings us back to where we started. The chosen day to begin the Olympic Games was selected according to traditional lucky numbers. At its most public moment, the Party and its government in Beijing have, in effect, conceded that they have stepped back from their commitment to wipe out superstition, and abandoned the communist belief that the demise of religion is only a matter of time—a relatively short time.

One of the biggest shifts in belief ever seen in the world has quietly taken place in China. Millions have abandoned the quasi-religious belief in Marxism. Sectors of the government, under the guise of economic development, now promote religious sites and activities. The collapse of utopian Marxism has meant the collapse of the

---

27. Gary Walker, 'A Special Day of Prayer', in *The Far East*, (July 2008): 20–21.
28. UCAN, 'Catholics Recite Pope's Prayer at Sheshan Marian Shrine on prayer day for China Church', (26 May 2008) at <www.ucannews. com/s008/05/26/catholics-recite-popes-prayer-at-sheshan-marian-shrne-on-prayer-day-for-china-church/>. Accessed 13 July 2008.

moral system which it had developed. The Party has been unable to find an effective substitute, despite the rhetoric of socialist ethics and socialist civilisation. Believers, including Christians, are now able to offer their own moral teaching in the public forum, to an extent that might not have been thought possible a decade ago. And as the number of believers increases, the government faces new issues of complexity of control, especially in the less formal areas of expression of belief, such as pilgrimages.

The future for religious belief does not depend on the policies of the Party or government in China. If we learn anything from the history of the last few decades, it is the astonishing survival of religious belief under the most difficult circumstances. But the way in which religious believers might be treated in the future is to a large extent in the hands of the Party and government. I have suggested that the legitimacy of the regime rests on four bases: its possession of the instruments of power, its capacity to deliver economic and social goods, its co-option of nationalist sentiment, and its success in preventing the emergence of any viable alternative. It is the last of these four which creates pressure on religions. Even the possibility that a religious group might provide a base for a challenger keeps the Party wary, and thus the Party keeps religious believers on a short leash.

And the Games? We now know that by the end of the first day of competition, China already led in the number of gold medals awarded. Perhaps the number eight really was a choice for good fortune.

Chapter Four

The Fifth Encounter Between Christianity and China: Only Persevering in Dialogue Can lead to Success

Jeroom Heyndrickx, cicm

Jeroom Heyndrickx, cicm

Four encounters between Christianity and China did not succeed

Historically the four encounters which have taken place between Christianity and Chinese culture, present a dramatic history! Today Christians in China still suffer the negative consequences of the failures of the past. However, in the past twenty-five years, the Chinese people have shown an increasing interest in Christianity, in ways never before experienced. Will this fifth encounter between Christianity and modern China succeed? While we can only speculate, it is very clear after so many failures, that the encounter will not succeed if the church turns back on the road of confrontation. Only by persevering in dialogue will the Christian faith find its home in the hearts and minds of the Chinese people. Both sides must liberate themselves from the old and fruitless traumas of the past. From the beginning of his pontificate Pope Benedict XVI has called for dialogue in the church in China: not the so-called 'patriotic' nor 'underground' 'churches', but simply the one, holy, catholic and apostolic church in China. The obvious question which looms large in this scenario is: Will the Chinese civil authorities agree and engage in this dialogue in sincerity and truth?

A history marked by confrontation and failed attempts to acculturate

When the Nestorians introduced the Bible into China in the seventh century, they strove to be guided by adaptation to Chinese culture and extant religious customs. Yet, due to historical situations in China, within two centuries the Nestorian Church was completely destroyed. In the seventh century, the Franciscans re-introduced Christianity into China and also strove to adapt the church to the culture of the Mongolians who ruled China at the time. Subsequently, again due to political turmoil, the Mongolian church was eradicated when the Ming Chinese expelled the alien Mongols from China. Thus two remarkable attempts to adapt Christianity to China failed.

During the seventeenth century the Jesuits were pioneers of dialogue in respect for Chinese culture and religions. Regrettably, what the Jesuits considered as valuable and totally acceptable in Chinese culture, the Dominicans and other missionary orders considered as pure superstition. Confrontation instead of dialogue now grew both *inside* the church and between the church and China as a cultured and civil society. This tragic confrontation caused Emperor Kangxi to withdraw his Edict of Tolerance, castigating Catholic faith officially as 'foreign' and 'not fit for China'.

This historic trauma rooted in confrontation and discord, continues to be a heavy cross borne by Chinese Christians as they strive to renew and develop their church as a fully acculturated and authentic expression of Christianity in China today. The Emperor's expulsion of the missionaries and suppression of the Catholic Church was the 'bitter fruit' of confrontation.

The fourth encounter between Christianity and China also brought shame upon the church during the nineteenth and twentieth centuries. Western colonial powers at that time exploited the weakness of China, which lead to the Opium War (1840). Haplessly, the church was involved in drafting the text of the Unequal Treaties between China and the colonial powers, and later became entirely controlled by the French Protectorate. As a result, the church was identified with the colonial imperialistic powers. This remained China's oft-repeated accusation against the church during the Cultural Revolution (1965–75) and even until today is exploited at China's convenience. Although China was never able to take revenge against England or France for their outrages, it raged against the church particularly on two occasions: once during the Boxer Uprising (1900) when thousands of Catholics and dozens of missionaries were murdered; and again during the Cultural Revolution (1965–1975) when radical slogans confirmed the cruel persecution, destruction and plundering of the church as vengeance for what happened during the nineteenth century. During that tragic era, church-state relations in China can only be described with the words 'confrontation' and 'conflict'.

Although the time of Mao Zedong, the Cultural Revolution, and even Marxism, belongs to the past in China, there is still an evident lack of religious freedom today. Nonetheless, at the same time, there is an undeniable acceptance of Christianity among the Chinese people, with an exceptional increase in both Catholic and Protestant believers. How shall China and the church deal with this new—the fifth—encounter between Christianity and Chinese culture and society? Both the church and the state have an historic responsibility to ensure that this fifth encounter should not fail. While it is unrealistic to expect that atheistic China and the Catholic Church might be friends, both carry with them the traumas of their own past, and both can only achieve stability and progress by putting an end to their old confrontational ways. Dialogue is the only way to these ends. Turning away from confrontation and persevering on the road of dialogue is the historic challenge which faces both the church and state in China at this historic juncture.

Vatican Council II: pioneer in promoting dialogue

Long ago the church was in conflict, and then in confrontation, with the world. But Since Vatican II the church has become a pioneer in the promotion of dialogue. In 1937, as Stalin sought to destroy the church, Pope Pius XI was prompted to use the harsh language of condemnation in his encyclical *Divini Redemptoris* ('Divine Redeemer'). Several years later an identical situation arose in China— both before and during the Cultural Revolution. Just ten days after Chinese authorities had defiantly ordered two bishops to be ordained without papal authorization, Pope Pius XII used condemnatory language in *Ad Apostolorum Principis* ('At the tomb of the prince of the Apostles'— March, 23, 1958). This became part of a more general situation of confrontation among the nations in the world which came to be known as the Cold War.

Nonetheless, history went on its course, and new situations evolved. In 1963 Pope John XXIII wrote *Pacem in Terris* ('Peace on Earth') in which he stressed that the church is open to different ideologies in the world. That was indeed a new ecclesial voice. In August 1964, at the beginning of the third session of Vatican II, Pope Paul VI wrote his important encyclical letter *Ecclesiam Suam* ('His Church') in which the word 'dialogue' appeared for the first time in an official church document. It meant the beginning of a new phase in church history. These calls for dialogue echoed an important discovery of Vatican II: namely, the need for the church to move with the times and to enter into dialogue with the world in response to emerging new global realities. While nations, religions and cultures were seemingly just discovering the need for dialogue, the church had been promoting such a move since the time of Pope John XXIII.

Dialogue: an essential element of evangelisation

During Vatican II the church came to understand that dialogue with the world is an essential element of evangelisation. This was a new insight for the church in her own mission. Evangelisation does not only consist in preaching the gospel; it presupposes that an essential dimension of such preaching is a willingness to learn from and be respectful of those who receive the message, the more so if those addressed are not only not our friends, but may even be outright opponents of the church. It might even happen that they remain opposed and that in a moment of confrontation, the content of the gospel message is rejected. Such confrontation, however, need not cause an outright conflict or rupture. Rather a challenge arises to both partners to pass beyond the confrontation and to search for a way to live together, even to work together for a common good without betraying the identity of either one. The fruit of this dialogue is then a peaceful and fruitful co-existence which portends a measure of real progress, compared to the negative consequences of confrontation and conflict. At this time in history the whole world, including the church, is undergoing a unique learning process from which there is no turning back. With every passing day, the irreversible process of globalisation signals ever more clearly the need to engage in dialogue in every sphere of human interaction—doing so with mutual appreciation among and between religions, cultures and states.

Promoting dialogue with China was a priority of the popes for forty years

Rapprochement and dialogue with the People's Republic of China has been a papal pre-occupation beginning with the reign of Paul VI, continued under John Paul II and continuing still with Benedict XVI. In 1970, two years before President Richard Nixon visited China, Pope Paul VI accompanied by the Vatican Secretary of State, Cardinal Cassarole, spoke during a stopover in Hong Kong, with solicitude and affection for China and the Chinese people. The same year Paul VI pleaded at an FAO meeting (UN Food and Agricultural Organization) to admit China as a member of FAO.

During his long pontificate, Pope John Paul II demonstrated a remarkable will to dialogue with China. He avoided all obstacles and setbacks and sidestepped all situations of confrontation. He acquiesced in offering a public apology, something that China had never obtained from the real imperialists—France, England, and Japan—apologising for whatever the church might possibly have done to offend China during the nineteenth century. China could hardly have asked for a greater incentive to enter into dialogue.

Yet China remained silent and has not effectively responded until today! Even though the church takes serious exception to situations where religious freedoms are denied in China, she still insists that confrontation is not an option. In January 2007, in an historic first, Pope Benedict XVI convened a China Consultation to discuss precisely these issues. The advice of the experts at this consultation was clear: to remain in a mode of dialogue, while avoiding confrontation with China. Benedict repeated this even more clearly in his Pastoral Letter to the church in China (June 30, 2007). In essence his message concludes: whoever would advocate today for confrontation with China ignores forty years of precedence and only thwarts all that has been achieved by the popes thus far in walking the road of constructive dialogue with China.

Promoting dialogue inside the church and with the government in China is delicate and demanding

In our cooperation as sister churches with the church in China, and in our contacts with civil authorities, we follow the guidelines of Pope Benedict XVI. His pastoral letter may be summarised in three elements: *engaging in dialogue, promoting reconciliation* and *building unity*. For several decades now, the church in China has sadly been divided into two communities. Each has opted for its own way to survive in a very complex and ambiguous Chinese situation, while remaining true to their Catholic faith. We believe, with Pope Benedict XVI, that both are indeed faithful and united with the universal church. We wish to loosen internal tensions, to encourage contacts between the two communities and by all means to avoid confrontation.

This task is delicate and demanding. It means first of all that Christians outside China remain in dialogue with both church communities, listening to both and *'in cari-tate et veritate'* (in charity and truth) trying to understand both. Those who opt for maintaining contacts with one or the other exclusively are acting against the guidelines of the pope. We cannot expect that Chinese Christians who suffered persecution for years and who are still ha-rassed today, should suddenly free themselves from old attitudes of confrontation and start speaking a language of dialogue. We should also fully understand that the ha-rassment which they undergo today only serves to con-firm them in their attitude of confrontation. Not surpris-ingly, they may even be irritated when those who have not endured their sufferings call upon them to be open and to enter into dialogue. This, however, should not be an excuse for those of us outside China to confirm them in their confrontational attitudes, for this would only serve to confirm the existing bitterness and further undercut the call of the pope to dialogue. We should rather draw their attention to the points touching upon the identity of our faith which the pope continually stresses as non-negotiable. While dialogue is the main line stressed by the Benedict XVI in the Pastoral Letter, it does imply an ele-ment of 'confrontation within the dialogue'.

It is precisely around these points of disagreement that we must search for a *modus vivendi* in the dialogue with civil authorities. It is a grievous distortion to isolate and cite this paragraph out of context, and thereby reduce the whole letter to a 'call to confrontation'! This is to betray the spirit and intent of the letter which is at heart a call for reconciliation, dialogue, unity. To encourage Christians in China today to speak the out-dated confrontational language of *Divini Redemptoris* is an anachronism. It only serves to confirm divisions inside the church and will lead the Catholic Church in China and civil authorities onto a dead-end street of confrontation and deepened animosity.

We must also try to understand those who, in line with the wish of the Pope, work in dialogue with civil authorities while remaining united with the Holy See. These people bear the heat of the day, while also suffering the opprobrium of those who misjudge their earnest intentions. On occasion we are perhaps shocked when one of them agrees to read a public statement imposed on him *per force*, seemingly questioning basic principles of the church. These people apparently judge, that in a situation of such un-freedom, they are justified in doing so. It is fruitless—and we would be guilty of rash judgement—to confront our brothers on these matters in the media. Rather we ought to strive to clarify the matter through personal contact and dialogue. Only frank communication with and understanding for both partners in the Chinese Church, will resolve the contradictions and bear fruit.

In this way, out of a seemingly hopeless division a 'united front of Christians' can grow, not in confrontation with the authorities, nor in the compromise of our identity in any way, but in dialogue towards developing a *modus vivendi* in respect for the identity of each. This will lead to a new situation replacing the confrontation and conflicts of the past. It is far more demanding but is more in line with Christian faith to dialogue frankly and try to solve disputes, rather than to encourage confrontation. Dialogue builds up while confrontation destroys.

The challenge of China and of the church is to remain engaged in dialogue

China and the church are both caught in a three-centuries-old confrontation which was exacerbated last century by the encyclical *Divini Redemptoris* and reached its dramatic peak during the Cultural Revolution. This confrontation produced deep mutual distrust from which both partners can free themselves only by a serious effort, yet this is the condition for dialogue. The fact that civil authorities in China are internally divided and adopt different approaches towards religion, complicates the situation. Even today some officials still speak of religion using expressions of the Cultural Revolution era while others promote the construction of a harmonious society. These declarations contradict each other. It is hard to imagine how the civil authorities can afford such internal divisions while so much social unrest grows daily in their country! Each time a local authority in China persecutes the church it creates a potential hotbed of unrest. By adopting a more reasonable attitude to solving problems of the church, the government would find in the church a partner for building a harmonious society.

Unfortunately incitement to confrontation coming from abroad offers these local officials an easy pretext to continue the persecution. Nevertheless, we hope that those who still opt for confrontation will not block those who follow the pope on the way of dialogue and cooperation. Christians in China expect more freedom of religion, yet perhaps we are not fully using the freedom to evangelise that already exists. Let us support the evangelisation projects that are in progress and not block them.

The letter of Pope Benedict XVI and the proposal to dialogue is an offer of the church. The atheistic government of China cannot afford to refuse this offer if it wishes to bring the situation of religious freedom in China to an internationally acceptable level. Meaningful recognition of Christianity by civil authorities and the establishment of unity inside the church in China would, in both instances, be an historic breakthrough, namely: a fifth and finally fruitful encounter between Christianity and China that would yield very positive benefits to both society and the church.

Chapter Five

Athens or Beijing?
Some Reflections on the
Possibilities of a Chinese Theology

Paul Rule

Paul Rule
Melbourne

When Tertullian made his famous remark, 'What has Athens to do with Jerusalem?' he was dismissing the use of Greek concepts to preach the good news originally revealed in Jewish terms. What he was contesting was the dominance of Greek thinking in the emerging church, a dominance which has continued to the present day.

In the notorious Regensburg address in September 2006 in which Pope Benedict made his remarks about Islam, misrepresented and misinterpreted in the media, he made some further comments which deserve, but have not received, more attention. He attacked the 'dehellenization' of theology and defended 'the thesis that the critically purified Greek heritage forms an integral part of Christian faith'. Note, not 'Christian theology' but 'Christian faith', thus appearing to claim that an orthodox Christian belief cannot be presented in other than Greek philosophical language. This view is contrasted by Benedict with Protestant biblicism and Harnack's programme of a return to the message of Jesus before it was perverted by, again to quote Benedict's pejorative characterisation, 'the accretions of theology and indeed of hellenization'.

Thus far, the critique by Benedict—or should we say Ratzinger, since he claimed in this lecture to be speaking as a theologian not as pope?—is clearly well founded. He is obviously correct in pointing to the historical role of Greek philosophy in the evolution of the church's self-understanding. In the process he does an injustice to Pascal in associating him with Harnack: Pascal's contrast of the God of the philosophers with the God of Abraham, Isaac and Jacob is not that of the biblical God with the God of theology, but of the God of direct religious experience with the God of systematic God-language. However, few historians of Christian theology would reject his basic claim that thinking in Greek has dominated its development.

It is his treatment of what he calls 'the third stage of dehellenization' that worries me. In an argument that first surfaced over twenty years ago in *The Ratzinger Report*,[1]

---

1. Joseph Cardinal Ratzinger with Vittorio Messori, *The Ratzinger Report: An Exclusive Interview on the State of the Church* (San Francisco: Ignatius Press, 1985).

Benedict opposes 'cultural pluralism' in theology. His argument is, of course, more sophisticated than Hilaire Belloc's 'The Faith is Europe. And Europe is the Faith'. It purports to be theological rather than simply historical. But as a simple historian with a longterm interest in things theological, especially as they relate to China, I would like to make what I consider to be some obvious comments.

Let us not be unfair to Benedict but quote his exact words:

> In the light of our experience with cultural pluralism, it is often said nowadays that the synthesis with Hellenism achieved in the early Church was a preliminary inculturation which ought not to be binding on other cultures. The latter are said to have the right to return to the simple message of the New Testament prior to that inculturation, in order to inculturate it anew in their own particular milieux. This thesis is not only false; it is coarse and lacking in precision. The New Testament was written in Greek and bears the imprint of the Greek spirit, which had already come to maturity as the Old Testament developed. True, there are elements in the evolution of the early Church which do not have to be integrated into all cultures. Nonetheless, the fundamental decisions made about the relationship between faith and the use of human reason are part of the faith itself; they are

developments consonant with the nature of faith itself.

There is again much that is obviously true in this. We now see that the Greek elements are there in not only the New Testament but the later Hebrew scriptures. But that does not privilege Greek thought over the perhaps even more prevalent Jewish terminology and theological themes in the bible. Jesus was a Jew, even if one living in a partly hellenized environment. And Jewish culture was 'eastern' rather than 'western' in its thought forms and socio-cultural assumptions. And note, again, his equation of 'human reason' with its Greek forms. Is there no rationality outside Athens? Did Plato's contemporaries, Confucius and the Buddha, and the Hebrew prophets, make no contribution to our rational understanding of the human condition?

In the last chapter of *The Ratzinger Report* the then Cardinal Ratzinger rejected pluralism in theology by focusing almost exclusively on Africa. Africa, he argued, has already been largely Europeanised. True, and so to some extent have China and India and just about anywhere else you might like to name. But to use the fact of an emerging global culture to deny continuing and underlying cultural difference is another matter. Global culture accretes as it grows, and the United States, its prime referent, is far from exclusively 'European'. We do not have a world language or if, in a sense, we do, it is not Greek, certainly not German, but English.

Quite frankly, I do not understand Benedict's references to preliminary inculturation and some sort of return to a pre- or non-cultural New Testament. I know of nobody in biblical studies who would regard the New Testament as a-cultural or mono-cultural, or in theology of religions who advocates abandoning the Christian heritage and starting anew as if it did not exist. But is Benedict not suggesting, even more than suggesting, that faith is primarily a matter of rationality, and rationality something exclusively Greek or, from some of his other statements since becoming pope, Greco-Roman?

Of course, there is no escaping philosophy in theology.[2] Although he was accused of doing so, Leslie Dewart in his influential books *The Future of Belief* and *The Foundations of Belief*[3] was not arguing for abandoning philosophical concepts and reasoning in theology. He was, however, in favour of 'dehellenising' which is not at all the same thing. Dehellenising is not a stripping away of the role of reason in theology, but an enriching through the exploration of non-Greek concepts and frameworks and their relevance to the understanding of the tradition.

Benedict's assumption is that the 'Greek' concepts of the creedal statements thrashed out by the early church councils are the guarantors of orthodoxy. But language

2. For an excellent treatment of this idea, see Jack Bonsor, *Athens and Jerusalem: the Role of Philosophy in Theology* (New York: Paulist Press, 1993).
3. Leslie Dewart, *The Future of Belief* (New York: Herder & Herder, 1966), *The Foundations of Belief* (New York: Herder & Herder, 1969).

and its comprehension change over time. Leaving aside another and legitimate complaint Benedict made in his Regensberg address about the hegemony of a scientific worldview which excludes the very possibility of language about the transcendent being intelligible, it must be admitted that the standard terminology of Catholic theology is misunderstood by most even well-educated Catholics. I would hazard a guess that for the great majority of them, the use of the terms 'person' and 'nature' in relation to the Trinity would be implicitly heretical since these terms now have, at least in English, meanings almost exactly the opposite to their classical usage. 'Relationship' is seen today as extrinsic not intrinsic or constitutive. And what does the language of 'substance' and 'accidents' in eucharistic theology mean to the scientifically educated whose models of physical reality have no place for such categories? Mouthing the correct words is no guarantee of orthodoxy.

I understand theological pluralism as the development of theologies using the language and assumptions of non-western civilisations. They would not supplant western theology, certainly not the great symbols of faith of the church councils, but explore other possibilities, other expressions of that faith, and their relationship with the traditional forms. To use the words of Confucius, there would be 'harmony without uniformity' (*Lunyu* 13:23). In a number of cases handled by Cardinal Ratzinger when head of the Congregation for the Doctrine of the Faith, notably those of Jacques Dupuis, Anthony de Mello and Tissa Balasuriya, the very legitimacy of such exploration was challenged. But to restrict theologising to European formulations in a church now numerically non-European is not only undesirable but, many would argue, impossible. And it would be a great loss to the church.

It also runs contrary to Benedict's plea to the bishops of Malaysia, Brunei and Singapore in June 2008:

> If the faith is to flourish, however, it needs to strike deep roots in Asian soil, lest it be perceived as a foreign import, alien to the culture and traditions of your people. Mindful of the manner in which Saint Paul preached the Good News to the Athenians (cf. *Acts* 17:22–34), you are called to present the Christian faith in ways that resonate with the 'innate spiritual insight and moral wisdom in the Asian soul' (*Ecclesia in Asia*, 6), so that people will welcome it and make it their own.[4]

How can this be done in the language of Athens?

Benedict XIV's strictures on 'interreligious dialogue' as 'putting the faith in parentheses' are well known but his support for 'intercultural dialogue' as an alternative is puzzling in the light of his earlier remarks.[5] How can intercultural dialogue be conducted exclusively in Euro-

---

4. Pope Benedict, 'Address of His Holiness Pope Benedict XVI to the Bishops of Malaysia, Brunei and Singapore on their "ad Limna" Visit', June 6 2008 at <http://www.vatican.va/holy_father/benedict_xvi/speeches/2008/june/documents/hf_ben-xvi_spe_20080606_bishops-malaysia_en.html>. Accessed 15 October 2009.
5. In a letter to Marcello Pera in November 2008 discussed in *Cath News* 24–28 November 2008.

pean terms? And how does this fit in with his predecessor's call for 'genuine interreligious dialogue' in *Ecclesia in Asia*?[6] In any case, in theology such thinking has been going on for half a century with some marked achievements. Asian theology is here to stay.

Nor is 'Asian theology' new. In the case of China various beginnings were made, some quite early in the history of modern Chinese Christianity. Taking up an idea mentioned in passing by Giulio Aleni SJ, Wang Zheng (1571–1644), a first generation convert, developed a theology of God as the 'Da Fumu', Great Father/Mother in his treatise *Weitian Airen Jilun*, 'A sublime discussion of the fear of Heaven and love of man' (1628). This is not some sort of feminist manifesto but a *xiao* (filiality) theology using filial relationship as its central focus. The Chinese Emperor was referred to as a 'Father/Mother', a parent embodying the stern but protective qualities of the father and the nurturing qualities of mother, and this image was used by Wang on a transcendent plane to refer to Heaven or The Lord of Heaven, the Christian God. The treatise was never published and its manuscript (in the Bibliothèque Nationale, Paris) unknown until recently.[7] But it suggests what might have been if this nascent 'Confucian Christianity' had not been stifled at the beginning of the eighteenth century by decisions from Rome.

Another area in which Confucianism might contribute to theology is its subtle and sophisticated treatment

---

6. Pope John Paul II, *Ecclesia in Asia* (New Delhi, 1999), V: 31.
7. v. Kai-tai Tony Wong, 'Wang Zheng's inculturated concept of God', in *Australian Journal of Mission Studies*, 2/1 (June 2008): 3–13.

of human nature (*renxing*). One late seventeenth-century Chinese Christian, Mathias Xia, wrote a treatise on the subject, again unpublished at the time.[8] It is just a sketch but it shows the potential of the Confucian treatment of the paradox of an originally good human nature and the patently bad behaviour of some humans in the explication of 'original sin'.

Another classical theological paradox is transcendence / immanence. In neo-Confucian philosophy the Supreme Ultimate, the transcendent source of all, is finally identified with *li*, immanent principle. I once asked the late Professor Julia Ching, an expert on Neo-Confucian philosophy and a Christian, whether she thought of God as immanent or transcendent, and she replied, not entirely in jest, 'I think of God as transcendent in the morning and immanent in the afternoon'. We must find ways of grasping the two together, of avoiding the dangerous dichotomies of God and nature that underpin much of our present ecological crisis. As one of the founding fathers of Neo-Confucianism, Zhang Zai, wrote on his study wall:

> Heaven is my father and Earth is my mother, and even such a small creature as I find an intimate place in their midst. Therefore that which fills the universe I regard as my body and that which directs the universe I consider

8. *Xing shuo* ['A Discussion of Human Nature'], manuscript in the Jesuit Roman Archives, Jap Sin I.135, published in facsimile in *Chinese Christian Texts from the Roman Archives of the Society of Jesus*, edited by Nicholas Standaert & Adrian Dudink (Taipei: Taipei Ricci Institute, 2002), 10: 1-16.

> my nature. All people are my brothers and
> sisters, and all things are my companions.
> The great ruler is the eldest son of my parents,
> and the great ministers are his stewards. Re-
> spect the aged—that is to treat them as elders
> should be treated. Show affection towards
> the orphaned and the weak—this is to treat
> them as the young should be treated. The sage
> identifies his character with that of Heaven
> and Earth, and the virtuous man is the best.
> Even those who are tired and infirm, crippled
> or sick, those who have no brothers or chil-
> dren, wives or husbands, are all my brothers
> who are in distress and have no one else to
> turn to …

There is much here in the Confucian notion of an ulti-
mately moral universe that might trigger useful theological thinking in the current ecological crisis.

And it is not just Confucianism that might lend Christian theology some new and appropriate concepts. When
that great Chinese Catholic thinker, John C Wu (1899–
1986), translated the New Testament he found in the key
Chinese concept of *dao* the ideal term to translate the Greek
logos in the beginning of John's Gospel. It is in many ways
much closer to the original than our ambiguous and weak
'Word'. Similarly in his *Beyond East and West*[9] and other
writings on the confluence of Christian and Daoist spiri-

---

9.   John Ching Hsiung Wu, *Beyond East and West* (New York: Sheed &
      Ward, 1951).

tualities, he explored ways in which Christianity might be enriched from this source.

And as well as spirituality, there is, of course, Confucian ethical and moral thinking, especially its humanist ethics, at once deeply rooted in a concept of humanity (*ren*) and humaneness (*ren*, same pronunciation and related ideograph) and founded in a transcendent source, *Tian* or Heaven. It was this that the first generation of Jesuit missionaries in China in the late sixteenth century, themselves deeply imbued in Christian humanism, found so attractive in the Confucian tradition. Matteo Ricci was to write of his conviction that 'the law of God was in conformity with the natural light [of reason] and with what their first sages taught in their books'.[10]

It is interesting to study the reaction of Chinese scholars to Matteo Ricci's attempt in his *Tianzhu Shiyi*[11] to expound Christian theology in Aristotelean terms. Most found it unintelligible. Some, however, were excited by this new way of thinking and applied it not only to their understanding of their new faith, but to problems of technology and government. And some attempted to relate these new ideas to their Neo-Confucian vocabulary and systems. It was not just a question of 'matching concepts', the method used in translating Buddhist sutras into Chinese, but of enriching both sides of the encounter by uncovering new implications and significance.

Many exercises in Asian theology are preliminary and

10. Matteo Ricci, *Fonti Ricciane*, edited by PM d'Elia, 3 vols (Roma: Liberia dello Stato, 1942–49), 1:195.
11. Matteo Ricci, *Tianzhu shyi*, edited by Douglas Lancashire et al (Taipei: Institut Ricci, 1985).

exploratory, but there have been some valuable studies of Hinduism and Buddhism in relation to Christian theology.[12] Sino-theology, however, is still in its very early stages, largely due to the situation of the Christian churches in the People's Republic of China. Nevertheless, it has enormous potential and I would like to conclude by indicating some of its possibilities.

Three thousand years of reflection on what it is to be human embodied in the Confucian tradition provide enormous resources for the kind of bottom-up anthropological theological thinking pioneered by Karl Rahner. The Chinese resistance to antagonistic dualisms and its favouring instead of harmonious reconciliations might be invaluable in resolving the crisis induced first in western and now in global society by binary thinking about mankind and nature. Here, one part of Benedict's programme outlined at Regensberg, his attack on atheistic scientism, might find an ally more potent than dichotomous hellenistic rationalism. And lastly, but perhaps most importantly, we might learn from China how to deal with what Panikkar calls 'the silence of God' in his treatment of Bud-

---

12. Some that come to mind are Raimundo Panikkar's *The Unknown Christ of Hinduism: Towards an Ecumenical Christophany*, revised edition (London: Darton, Longman & Todd, 1981) and *The Silence of God: The Answer of the Buddha* (Maryknoll NY: Orbis Books, 1989); John B Cobb Jr, *Beyond Dialogue: Toward a Mutual Transformation of Christianity and Buddhism* (Philadelphia: Fortress Press, 1982); *The Emptying God: A Buddhist-Jewish-Christian Conversation*, edited by JB Cobb Jr and C Ives (Maryknoll, NY: Orbis Books, 1990); and John P Keenan, *The Meaning of Christ: A Mahayana Theology* (Maryknoll NY: OrbisBooks, 1989).

dhism, and the *Dao De Jing* refers to as the 'Way (*Dao*) that cannot be spoken of'.

To close off such possibilities in the name an orthodoxy (a nice Greek word) once and for all embodied in Greek categories would be to diminish Christianity and especially the Catholicity of the Catholic Church.

Chapter Six

Buddhism and the Religious Awakening of China

Benoît Vermander SJ

Benoît Vermander SJ
Taipei Ricci Institute
Taipei
Taiwan

During the last decades, China's religious awakening has manifested itself in many ways. One of its most notable expressions has been the rapid development of Buddhism, based on the reconstruction and expansion of the Buddhist monastic communities.[1] These communities are

---

1. Christian Cochini has published a *Guide des temples boudhistes de Chine* (Paris: les Indes savantes, 2007), introducing in great detail 200 Buddhist temples and monasteries. An English edition of this Guide is due for publication in 2009, under the auspices of the Macao Ricci Institute.

nowadays some of the most notable and organised forces of the civil Chinese society.

This is not surprising; from the very beginning of Buddhist expansion in China, the monastic community constitutes the axis around which rotate the devotional practices, the beliefs and the institutional continuity of Buddhism. A liturgical place, the temple acts as a collective intercessor for the community of believers directing to it their wishes and their prayers, especially for the deceased. As places of learning, the great temples make it possible to carry on through several centuries the translation of the Buddhist canon into Chinese, one of the greatest editorial enterprises of history, and to multiply the interpretations of it. As a place of power, the temple knows how to negotiate its relationship with the political leaders of the locality and then of the Empire, although this model was held at bay at the time of the big persecution of the ninth century, partly due to the concentration of wealth realised by the monastic communities. The best summary of the *modus operandi* proper to Chinese Buddhism is provided by Erik Zürcher:

> During the first three centuries of our era the dissemination of Buddhism in China was carried on at the popular level. In the 4th century, Buddhism starts reaching out to the elites, and, about 400, the first large monasteries are established. Enriched by important donations, they keep developing by running social and economic activities: management of their estates, accumulation of capital, organization

of fairs and pawn shops, printing press and guest houses.

Chinese Buddhism has thus become a powerful religious power drawing its strength from this remarkable institution which is the monastery. But the amazing fact is that this great religious power came to pass without any form of central direction or coordination. Chinese Buddhism has always been an ocean of countless centers, big and small, of very different levels, the biggest ones sponsored by the Court and peopled with learned monks, the smallest ones vegetating in the villages and inhabited by some illiterate monks. In summary: a great institutional force, combined with a great weakness of organization.[2]

The reconstruction of Chinese Buddhism after the turmoil of the Cultural Revolution relied therefore on the monastic institution, as it was already the case in other times. And the vitality of the monasteries bears witness to that of the Buddhist practices and beliefs in the whole of the society. Interestingly, it is perhaps the second part of Zürcher's statement, on the organisational weakness of the Buddhist network, which turns out to be less relevant for the present period. This is because of the characteristics of the structure of the Party-State: the recognition of the role of the Chinese Buddhist Association and the

---

2. Erik Zürcher, *Bouddhisme, Christianisme et société Chinoise* (Paris: Julliard, 1990), 26–27.

concomitant creation of 'transmission belts' between the Power and the local religious organisations go hand in hand with a greater communication and solidarity between the various centres, big or small, which, taken as a whole, innervate Chinese Buddhism. In other words, Chinese Buddhism seems to be more robust and more interdependent today than at any time in the past.

It is not so easy to describe the Chinese Buddhist world in its totality. Monks and nuns, be they still novices or already ordained, are as easily identified by their clothing, their tonsure, and, for those who have been ordained, by their ordination certificates as by the scars on the head following the fulfilled rites. But the faithful are not recognisable in the crowd of those who visit the temples, so great is the diversity of their motivations and behaviours. The quality of 'Buddhist faithful' (*jushi*) is normally reserved for those who have formally taken refuge (*guiyi*) in the 'three Jewels' (The Buddha, the Law, the Community). In return they receive a certificate which they can show at the entrance of a temple to be exempted from paying admission fees, for instance, or to get board and lodging. The levels of membership are many and not always so clearly identified.

The visitor to a Buddhist monastery will generally be struck by the predominance of young monks, often already at the head of their monasteries, sometimes graduated from prestigious universities. These monks are more and more engrossed in their tasks—construction of buildings, setting up of research centres and libraries in social institutions. The production of this elite of clerics is facilitated by regulations reserving admission into Buddhist studies centres to those of less than thirty years of age on average. Beside these young monks, one will usually see some quite old and silent monks who had entered the monasteries at a very young age, and long before the turmoil of the sixties. Having already assimilated the spirit and traditions of the school to which their temple belonged, and managing to survive, even starting anew some communities at the beginning of the eighties, they had handed over their responsibilities to their successors.

Of course, with the passing of time, the absence of an intermediary generation, conspicuous between 1985 and 2000, is less visible now, and the generation in power today has progressively asserted its experience and its authority. The nature and the exercise of this authority depends mostly on a transformation in the economic bases of the monasteries. The exploitation of the agricultural estates was replaced by an increased dependence on donations (at first from overseas, then from local donors), on the help of government agencies (for the reconstruction of buildings in particular), on the practice of rituals, and on some specialised productions. The monks affiliated to a given monastery generally receive a modest allowance, in nature or in cash, in return for their liturgical talents or by other services.

One cannot understand the present state of Chinese Buddhism by looking only at its two extremes—the time of its beginnings, when the basic shape of the monastic community has taken form, and the reconstruction boom of the last two or three decades. One must also say a word about the ups and downs of its history throughout the last 150 years, for the destructions of the Cultural Revolution had been preceded by those of the Taiping Rebellion (1851–1864), particularly in South China, the traditional Buddhist bastion. The subsequent effort of reconstruction coincided then with rising internal criticisms concerning the system of formation and the (non) effective aspects of precepts. Chinese Buddhism was entering the era of the *aggiornamento*. Some of the reformer monks advocated mainly going back to the ancient disciplines, privileging a small number of select texts and practices of meditation. A little later, came another trend, of which the monk Taixu (1890–1947) is the most well known representative. This involved a modernisation of Buddhism, following a method close to that of the Chinese Republicans of the beginning of the last century—the ideal 'science and democracy' applied, so to speak, to the religious sphere. The role of the laity was emphasised and monastic education was similar in style to that of the western universities.

The creation, in the first half of the twentieth century, of the Chinese Buddhist Association, the popularisation of a 'humanistic Buddhism' or 'Buddhism in the world' (*renjian fojiao*), the contacts between monks and political leaders of that time—all these characteristics have probably helped shape the look of Chinese Buddhism when it recovered relative freedom of movement after 1980. Nonetheless, the debates which characterised the revival of 1870–1940 continue today, as the Buddhist community seeks to define its relationship with a post-modern China in a state of constant transformation.

Neither the development of Chinese Buddhism today, nor its social and cultural impact, can be understood without resituating it within the more general context of the religious awakening of China. Of course, the question of the nature of the 'religious' in China has to be raised at once, and therefore the question of its 'awakening'. In China, as it is commonly said, religion affects and is affected by everything surrounding it. Rites, pilgrimages, temples, congregations, and beliefs create a landscape where political, civilian and familial institutions are inextricably linked together in a whole through which the community reproduces and regulates itself, and at the same time expresses a search for meaning and prosperity.

The permanence and centrality of the role of the Emperor in Chinese religion would have created an obstacle to the emergence of the religious sphere as a specialised social agency understood in the sense known by the western world. It must also be emphasised that the very word 'religion' (*zongjiao*), in the Chinese language is relatively new, a term borrowed from the Japanese language towards the end of the nineteenth century to express a reality which could not be found in the Chinese world. From this perspective, to speak of the 'return of the religious' would be immediately questionable.

However, the above analysis fails to recognise that China has experienced a progressive structuring of the religious sphere, and a historical analysis of the 'birth of the religious' in China makes it possible to correct the excessively 'essentialist' aspect of the previous approach. When the scholars of the 1920s and 1930s affirmed that 'China [did] not need religion', they acknowledged by the same token the distinction between the sphere of the religious and the other spheres of social activity—an evolution carried on through quite a few centuries. In other words, Chinese religions are historical phenomena in perpetual evolution, redefinition and social specialisation. Religions have developed with, against and beside the state; dogmas and norms of behaviour have been asserted, questioned and developed. China was shaped and transformed by religious passions and institutions, in a context of inter-religious dimension.

Thus, to speak of a return of the religious amounts to positioning oneself in the continuity of history. After being stalled at the time of the Sino-Japanese war, the debate about the role of religious beliefs and institutions in individual and social life was revived during the period of reform and opening in 1979.There was also a revival of the interaction between religions which are both accomplices and rivals—a type of debate and interaction that were characteristics of the period which had immediately followed the first Chinese revolution. Such social autonomy of the religious sphere was in some ways a sign of China's entrance into modernity, and similar issues are at stake today.

Towards 1979, most observers thought that religious beliefs and groups had been eradicated from Chinese territory. Ten years of Cultural Revolution had brought about the destruction of popular temples, Christian churches, Buddhist monasteries, the persecution of all clerics and the death of many of them. In the period immediately preceding this, the severe framing of 'official' religions by 'patriotic associations', transmission belts of the Party, as well as the interdiction of any contact with foreign people had already severely reduced the religious space. Policies of reform and opening rebuilt, therefore, a limited and controlled space for official religions: the Bureau of Religious Affairs sees to it that local groups do not threaten public order and patriotic associations guarantee that the ideological conformity of public positions taken by religions. But inside the reestablished monasteries, old monks who have returned from the countryside can resume monastic life and receive novices; local Catholic congregations receive religious candidates; churches reopen to cult; Taoist pilgrimages start again . . . There would be therefore today about one hundred million Buddhists, twenty to thirty million Moslems, fifteen million Protestants registered with the official structures (and perhaps up to fifty million avoiding the official statistics), twelve to fifteen million Catholics belonging to the 'patriotic' and 'underground' churches. There are no statistics regarding either the number of Taoist faithful or those of the believers of 'new religions' or of the cults of ethnic minorities. The religious penetration is not measured only by the number of faithful and buildings. The 1980s also see the surging of a 'cultural fever', which goes along with the renewal of the study of religious texts and the interest in ascetic and liturgical practices. The religious awakening of China is shown not only by the fact that the number of believers of any obedience has surpassed that of the members of the Party, but by a quest for meaning conveyed by religious questions and texts, beyond confessional belonging.

The 'growth crisis' of the religions is in fact its real awakening. The religious awakening goes beyond mere curiosity or individual adhesion; it expresses itself by the search for a new articulation between belief and society, by the creation of a public or semi-public space in which can occur collective expressions of faith. Therefore one notices less a religious *restoration* than a religious *transformation*, inseparable from the social and cultural transformation which is going on. Religions in China are *henceforth* wondering what might be their pertinence, they are conscious of being agents of the best aspects of the cultural tradition of this country and responsible in their role for influencing the way China makes a contribution to today's world. The question of the pertinence of the various religious forms matches the question of their universality: is it sufficient for a religious expression to call itself 'Chinese religion', or is it the universal character of the values and outlook expressed by this religion that authenticates its pertinence?

According to the opinion of the majority of observers, and this in spite of the difficult interpretation of statistics, the two religions whose growth is today the fastest in China are obviously Buddhism and Christianity. Such growth is multiform, and must not hide the weaknesses, the divisions and the contradictions within these believing communities. The question of the stature and of the influence of Tibetan Buddhism with respect to Han Buddhism will mark the next development of the first of these two religions. And the influence of the evangelical groups, or, on the contrary, of the syncretistic ones, within Catholicism as well as within Protestantism, will determine the final relation between Christianity on one hand, and Chinese society and power on the other one— Christianity being perceived by the authorities with more suspicion than a Buddhism reputed to be more 'national' and politically accommodating. But still, it is the very interaction between these two religions which will also exert its influence on the future outlines of the Chinese civilian society, reducing it to a series of juxtaposed communities, mutually ignoring the groups nearby, or favoring mutual understanding and interfaith collaboration. If both expressions of belief, as one may assume, go beyond the present stage of their growth crisis, if both can assert themselves as authentically 'Chinese' and nevertheless universal religions, their interaction will determine how China takes part in cultural globalisation.

Chapter Seven

Chinese Protestant Christianity: A Reappraisal

Justin Tan

Justin Tan
Melbourne

During a conversation with a local church leader in Beijing, Thomas Harvey, a reporter, the author of the recent biography of Wang Mingdao, a well-known patriarch of the Chinese church, inadvertently strikes on the right chord of the dichotomy of the progress of the Protestant church in Modern China. He was trying to understand the ethos of the Chinese church today. The answer from the Chinese leader is: 'Understand two men, and you will understand Chinese Christianity.' Asked the reporter, 'Which two?' The answer was, 'Wang Mingdao and KH Ting'.[1]

---

1. Thomas Alan Harvey, *Acquainted with Grief: Wang Mingdao's Stand*

The surge in the number of Christian believers from the 1980's onward is bewildering to those still holding to the secular atheistic socialist ideology.[2] The landscape of Chinese Christianity is changing so fast that whatever is said about it will have to keep pace with the latest development. We will start with the above comment.[3]

The history of Protestant mission in China has been well documented, so there is no need for us to deliberate too much on it here. Jessie Lutz, for example, gives a broad perspective in her essay, 'China and Protestantism: Historical Perspective, 1807–1949'.[4] She accurately points out that, 'Chinese generally neglected the history of Christianity in China or viewed Christian missions as the cultural form of Western imperialism'.[5] That was true for the

---

for the Persecuted Church in China (Grand Rapids: Brazos Press, 2002), 7.

2. Leung Ka-lun, *The Rural Churches of Mainland China Since 1978* (Hong Kong: Alliance Bible Seminary, 1999) [in Chinese], 20; Leung here quotes a researcher of religions in China, Lo Zhu-feng, from his 1988 book.

3. Much of what transpired in the history of the modern Chinese church is discussed in the other articles in this issue, and it would be futile to repeat them here. This article is based on the material mentioned in the other articles and attempts a fresh reflection on the situation in the Chinese church today. A note: Due to time constraints I have been unable to expound on the major ideas I discuss and I apologise for some sweeping statements in this article. I hope to correct this by producing a more detailed investigation at a later stage.

4. Jessie G. Lutz, 'China and Protestantism: Historical Perspectives, 1807–1949', in *China and Christianity: Burdened Past, Hopeful Future,* edited by Stephen Uhalley Jr and Xiaoxin Wu (NY: M.E. Sharpe, 2000), 179–93.

5. Lutz, 'China and Protestantism', 179.

period she is investigating. But she also accurately points out that Western studies of Christianity in China have by and large concentrated on the impact of the mission and missionaries on the Chinese society and religious realm.[6] We will endeavour to analyse it from the perspective of the Chinese Christians.

The Chinese viewed the missionary enterprise differently. The early converts were not as strong in their stance, and saw their faith as just an alternative to the prevailing indigenous faiths around them. They were not highly regarded by society as a whole, and because the missionary enterprise was tinged with political aggression, though not entirely of its own doing, it was thus thought to be associated with Western imperialism. Although there were

---

6. A good example is found in the article by Ryan Dunch, who insists in seeing almost every subsequent movement as an extension of the missionary enterprise, and thus produces a flawed account of the Chinese Protestant Church today. See Ryan Dunch, 'Protestant Christianity in China Today: Fragile, Fragmented, Flourishing', in *China and Christianity*, 195–216. Dunch harks back to the early twentieth-century version of Protestantism and views the present situation as either diverting or conforming to the missionary enterprise from that period. Thus he sees no 'new' indigenous churches except those which deviate from the 'orthodox' teaching of the early missionaries, which by the way are condemned by local Chinese Christians as cults anyway. There is a need to at least segregate the Christian message and the Christian church from what Dunch sees as the teaching of the missionaries. Of course, most of the teaching would probably be derived from the missionaries, but the Chinese accepted the Christian message even in the midst of being accused of linking with Western powers. They nonetheless tried desperately to make Christianity their own, and history has shown that they have partly succeeded.

some genuine converts, many were attracted to the faith by the offer of material benefits and some because of their disdain for the fallacy of folk religions. Many embraced 'the concept of a loving and forgiving Jesus in the light of personal troubles and social disorder'.[7]

This was to change when, despite the upheaval of both the Boxer Uprising and The Anti-Christianity Movements of the early twentieth century, Chinese intellectuals began to embrace the Christian faith in greater number.[8] They began to accept the progress of the West with its Christian heritage, and thus saw Christianity as one of the ideas that would bring China into the modern world. Lutz summarises it well: 'Variety within the protestant community increased; conservative, evangelical, societies strengthened their presence; the social gospel approach gained momentum, and Chinese formed their own faith sects and autonomous churches'.[9]

---

7. Lutz, 'China and Protestantism', 182.
8. Edmond Tang, a Catholic, bypasses the intensely lively period of the Protestant attempt at contextualisation when he says, 'It is my conviction that never before in recent Chinese history, since the time of Matteo Ricci, has Chinese society been as open to Christianity as today' (quoted by Gianni Criveller in the article in this issue). He is of course talking about 'openness', but although the Protestant church had encountered opposition in the early decades of the twentieth century, it is much more 'open' to Christianity than in the age of Matteo Ricci, who only worked with the official class. The Protestant movement is much more wide-ranging. Jessie Lutz even called it 'Christianity's golden age in China' (Lutz, 'China and Protestantism',187).
9. Lutz, 'China and Protestantism', 187.

The progress to autonomy was slow, however, due to the fact that, 'Western mission boards and many missionaries were reluctant to relinquish the power of the pocket book, which gave them a decisive voice in most matters of importance'.[10] Strangely enough, this attitude was both detrimental and served the progress of the protestant church at the same time: detrimental, because it has left an indelible stain of the perceived imperialism on the protestant church, which was viewed as being controlled by Western powers for motives other than religious; serving the progress, because it was this disdain for the control that accelerated the growth of indigenous churches which began to mushroom all over China. Missionaries tend to label this growth as heretical and 'cultish'. True, there were quite a few cults which were fiercely against the stranglehold of the missionaries and taught doctrines which deviate from orthodoxy,[11] but many indigenous churches were established based on the conservative evangelical line. A case in point is obviously Wang Mingdao.

Although the churches founded under Wang Mingdao were few in numbers, his conservative evangelical stance was very much admired. He was but one of the leaders who held to the separation of faith and political power in the climate in which he lived, but his approach served the conservative protestant church well beyond his time. During Wang's time, he was even held out as an example

---

10. Lutz, 'China and Protestantism', 189.
11. True Jesus Church (Zhen Yesu Jioahui), founded in 1917, is a case in point.

to imitate.[12] Meanwhile a gradual distancing from the missionary enterprise has already begun, due in part to some progressive missionaries advocating the surrender of control to the local leaders and starting the process of training them to take up important posts in the church, and in part to the anti-Christian (hence anti-missionary) sentiments that we mentioned above. The period between the height of the anti-Christianity movements of the 1920's and the Second World War, and eventually Communist rule of 1949, saw the waning of influence of Westerners and strongly indigenous, evangelical movements gained ground. Although they still held to the separation of faith and political power, foreign aggression and civil unrest meant that they would have to take sides in the direction of patriotism. Most would declare their loyalty to the Motherland, through external protests of aggression and internal search for Christianity with a Chinese face.[13]

It was also at this time that the Protestant church experienced revival throughout China. One could see this

---

12. Lutz indicates that rejection of the missionary hierarchy elicited admiration even among some nationalistic youth by leaders such as Wang and Song Shangjie (sic); see 'China and Protestantism', 189.

13. References are many and varied; see, for example, the following articles in *Christianity in China: From The Eighteenth Century to the Present*, edited by Daniel H Bays (Stanford: Stanford University Press, 1996); Peter Chen-Main Wang, 'Contextualizing Protestant Publishing in China: The Wenshe, 1924–1928', 292–303; Daniel H Bays, 'The Growth of Independent Christianity in China, 1900–1937', 307–16; and especially, Timothy Brook, 'Toward Independence: Christianity in China Under the Japanese Occupation, 1937–1945', 317–37.

as converts looking for hope and comfort through religion, but is also a strong elements of pride and courage as the church enjoyed its first taste of maturity and
independence. Self-support and self-rule meant that the
believers were becoming bold and taking the evangelistic task as their own responsibility, so it was just a matter of time before growth came. Revival meetings were
held by Chinese leaders like Song Shangjie (John Sung)
and Ni Tuosheng (Watchman Nee), and they were reap-
ing much greater harvest in terms of numbers than Western missionaries. Had the political situation remained
unchanged, we would probably have seen the greatest
growth and openness towards Christianity ever. Some
older believers today still reminiscence over the sacrifice
of the Western missionaries and are indeed grateful for
their audacity in bringing the gospel to China, but these
deeds are now only a matter of historical record.

Wang Mingdao's stand on the freedom of Christianity
to self-propagate and his fierce defiance against foreign
powers from both in the form of the Western mission-
ary-led control of the church and the Japanese invasion
earned him a place in the heart of the Christians when the
church later encounter in the 1950s the persecution under
the new regime.

In the theological realm, the revival adhered to the
conservative, evangelical stance of spiritual experience
of rebirth through repentance and belief in the salvation
of Christ (many would add the doctrine of 'once saved
always saved'), hope in the form of pre-millennialism,
the sanctifying power of the Holy Spirit (the pentecos-
tal influence has remained strong especially in the rural

churches); the ethical principle of love of neighbour; the evangelistic effort as a duty of the believers and of course the separation of faith and political power. This helped to set the tone for the protestant church of the future, so much so that when the next wave of revival came in the late twentieth century, the theology was firmly adhered to.

On the other side of the spectrum is the so-called 'Social gospel' movement in the by and large denominational churches. The movement was equally critical of the control of Western missionaries, but saw the vocation of the Church as *jiu guo* (rescuing the nation). The contextualisation of the Christian message came in terms of its social and political responsibilities. The program of spiritual evangelisation had been taken over by the agenda for social reform. Primary was the program to educate the Chinese for nation building in Christian-based tertiary institutions like Yenjing University. Academics like Zhao Zichen and Liu Tingfang championed liberal theology from the 1920s to the 1940s, and accused the conservative evangelical churches of being too inward looking and therefore of little impact to the rapidly changing China. This has indeed dichotomised the protestant church. The conservatives coined the label: *bu xin pai* (the Unbelief Party), to describe the liberals who tampered what they saw as the true essence of the Christian faith. But it is also true that both sides have the well-being of the Chinese nation in mind. The conservatives saw the gospel as the only moral way of reforming China (*fu yin jiu guo*, only the gospel can save China), and the liberals saw the ethos of Christianity as the principle for their social program.

The situation came to a head under the new regime from 1949, with the founding of the Three-Self Patriotic Movement (TSPM) under Wu Yaozong (YT Wu),[14] one of the most controversial Christian figures at this period: 'Wu represented an important sector, the urban Christian intellectuals who insisted on a strong social and political relevance for Christianity and who were willing to participate in the state-supervised institutions devised to manage religious affairs'.[15]

Wu's stance on Christianity as a religion of love changed with the Japanese Invasion of World War II. He advocated ethics of coercion in the midst of oppression and felt that this was still in line with the ethics of Jesus.[16] The change served him well from then on. The logical

---

14. There is no need to go into details here as it is widely discussed in monographs concerning this period of the Protestant Church. Suffice it to say that the controversy of the Three-Self Movement has been going on for sixty years and shows no sign of consensus. We refer to two opposing views in two books: Philip L Wickeri, *Seeking the Common Ground: Protestant Christianity, the Three-Self Movement and China's United Front* (Maryknoll: Orbis Books, 1988) and Ying Fuk-tsang and Leung Ka-lun, *The Three-Self Patriotic Movement in 1950s* (Hong Kong: Alliance Bible Seminary, 1996) [in Chinese]. Again, Wu Yaozong has been the subject of two opposing portraits: see Gao Wangzhi, 'YT Wu: A Christian Leader Under Communism', in *Christianity in China*, edited by Bays, 338–52 and Leung Ka-lun, *Wu Yaozong San Lun* (Hong Kong: Alliance Bible Seminary, 1996) [in Chinese]. Recently there has been an entirely sympathetic portray of Wu and his theological stance in 'Christianity in China: Contextual Wisdom', in *Judujiao Zai Zhongguo: Chujing Hua De Zhihui*, edited by Zhao Shi-lin and Duan Qi, two volumes (Beijing: Zongjiao Wenhua, 2009) [in Chinese], vol 2, 417–527.
15. Lutz, 'China and Protestantism',190.
16. *Judujiao Zai Zhongguo*, 434–42.

conclusion is the transformation of society through social reconstruction, toppling the oppressive imperialistic elements and advocating socialism.[17] He said in no uncertain term that, 'we can at least say that socialism is better suited than capitalism in advocating Christianity's respect for the spirit and value of humanity'.[18] He then adamantly stated that the current emphasis on personal salvation, avoiding the reality of the oppression of the people, only confirmed the slogan: 'religion is the opiate of the people'. To avoid this degrading fate, Christianity needed to join forces with socialism for social reconstruction and to do battle against oppressive forces.

Wu set the tone for the theological reconstruction of the Three-Self organisation. He endorsed in its entirety the program of the Western liberal social gospel agenda, critiqued all major dogmas of the orthodox evangelical church, including the divinity of Christ, the doctrine of Trinity that derived from that, and the uniqueness of the Gospel message.[19] As it turns out, his theological stance served his socialist agenda well. This was carried over to the TSPM, and from its inception, it has strongly stood against the orthodox evangelical church, accusing it of being non-productive and anti-social. But the battleground had shifted since liberation, the prophetic voice of the

---

17. *Judujiao Zai Zhongguo*, 443–54.
18. *Judujiao Zai Zhongguo*, 445, quoting Wu's 1939 article.
19. *Judujiao Zai Zhongguo*, 445–83. Duan Qi unwittingly admits to all that the conservative Christians accused Wu of one of '*buxin pai*', which holds that none of the orthodox doctrines are sacred ground.

church was replaced by the 'salt and light' ethics[20] of good citizenship. Christians should, as far as possible, conform to the policy of the state and make haste to assist in the reconstruction of society and state. Since socialism was viewed as the best possible political system, Christians should wholeheartedly embrace this state policy.

Wu's stance was carried through to the letter in the TSPM by his successor, Bishop Ting. Ting was persuaded by Wu to return to China while still a radical Christian student leader in 1949. Come 1951 Ting became actively involved in the work of TSPM. From its founding in 1954 until the end of the Cultural Revolution, TSPM had indeed tread on very sensitive ground; it had an unenviable position of positively endorsing the principle that all organisations including the religious should be conformed to the socialist agenda, hence negatively foretelling the eventual demise of all religions when a socialist society is realised, and pragmatically maintaining its operation of the 'three-self's. Denominational churches which had links with the West were eventually shut down, and but for the strong plea of the TSPM all would have gone. It was an understatement to say that the church suffered and was nearly crushed through this tumultuous period of the so-called leftist inclination.[21] Throughout this period Bishop Ting stoically maintained his stance and did what little he could to retain at least the church's survival

---

20. Alluding to Jesus' call for believers to be 'the Salt and Light of the World'.
21. Modern interpreters of this period would place the blame of the suffering of the church squarely on the Left; see for example, the articles in *Judujiao Zai Zhongguo*.

mode. It is almost inevitable that the hostility between TSPM and those Christians who were forced underground grew to monstrous proportions.

Theologically, Ting and by default the TSPM still hold to the liberal agenda. TSPM was essentially under political control in the years of the Cultural Revolution, Ting and his cohorts were heard to comment on occasions that religions had virtually disappeared according to the socialist agenda. History has indeed proved him wrong, the ideal of a communist society were far from being achieved, but religious fervour became the talk of the day.[22] However, this would come later, meanwhile the protestant church was almost brought to its knees, gradually at first in the 1950s and 1960s, and rapidly during the tumultuous years of the Cultural Revolution.[23] The conservative wing of the protestant church was forced underground, blaming and distancing itself from TSPM for co-operating with the authorities. But 1980 saw the rehabilitation of TSPM's role in Protestant religious affairs. Ting was elected chair of both TSPM and CCC (China Christian Council). Ting's position remained unchanged since his mentor Wu Yaozong. But the openness towards religions was now very much in evidence. Since 1980 according to one report, nearly 50,000 churches opened their doors for worship, seven-

---

22. Fuk-tsang Ying, 'Mutual Adaptation to Socialism: TSPM and Church-State Relations', in *China and Christianity: A New Phase of Encounter?* edited by Felix Wilfred, Edmond Tang, and Georg Evers, *Concilium* 2008/2: 71.

23. Zhao Shi-lin simply stated that, 'During the Cultural Revolution, Protestant Christianity was severely damaged', in *Judujiao Zai Zhongguo*, 538.

ty per cent of these are newly built, nineteen seminaries were reopened with more than 10,000 students, not to mention the vast publications of religious materials, especially through the work of the Amity Fund.[24]

On numerous occasions Ting restated the unchanging task of TSPM, except to add that it should be done well (the so-called *'san hao'*). On this, he advocated an overhaul of theological reconstruction with Chinese characteristics. Instead of the orthodox protestant position of 'justification by faith', he himself proposed the so-called 'justification by love'.[25] The essence of God is love, the love that embraces all, including believers and non-believers, whose aim it is to do good and bring welfare to humanity. He advocates what he calls the 'Cosmic Christ', who is willing to join in the process of creating a harmonious world, with whomever aspire to work towards this end. He is adamant that justification by faith has its fallacy in only catering for people who believe but behave atrociously, and disregarding those who are non-believers who have contributed much to society.[26] The fact of the incarnation

---

24. *Judujiao Zai Zhongguo*, 541.
25. All Ting's major works are collected in his *Ding Guangxun Wenji* (Nanjing: *Yilin chubanshe*, 1998).
26. In The Proceedings of the Chinese Christian Academic Seminar on Views of Scripture in 2000, he uses historical figures to illustrate this: 'This [justification by faith] seems at first sight like a question of faith, but taken further it is a question of political attitude. If all believers go to Heaven, well, Chiang Kai-shek was a believer, so he must be in Heaven, sitting at the right hand of God. But Chairman Mao, Liu Shaoqi, Deng Xiaoping, Zhou Enlai, Lei Feng: none of them was a believer, so they must all have gone to Hell. Isn't this a matter of political attitude?' Quoted by Fuk-tsang Ying, 'Mutual

is to embrace the culture that Christ was born into: 'Incarnation needs the motherhood of Mary, so it is that Chinese Theology needs the motherhood of Chinese Culture'.[27] The theology of the love of God corresponds with the Chinese value of *ren-ai*. So love can become the ethical basis of all Christian behaviour, political and social. It is true that before socialism became a reality, religion *was* the opiate of the people, but since then, Christianity has coincided with the socialist ideal. Ting puts it this way: 'My belief in the love of God and that China should go the way of socialism are one, it is mutually strengthening. Socialism precisely utilises love to organise the masses.'[28] The very non-orthodoxy of Ting's reading of Christian faith is the mainstay of TSPM. This is wholehearted rejected by most of the leaders of the conservative non-state Church.

The search for the reasons for the phenomenal growth of the Protestant Church since the end of the Cultural Revolution has been going on, both within China and without. TSPM would like to think that it was because of their perseverance that the Chinese church could survive at all, and see growth as the church meeting the need o people looking for meaning and vision in the era of open and reform policy of the Chinese Communist Party. The other factor put forward is that Christianity in China has finally shed its foreign imperialist façade and wholeheartedly embraced the patriotic social reconstruction agenda. This has caused a surge in the big interest and above all

---

Adaptation to Socialism: TSPM and Church-State Relations', 81.
27. Ting, *Ding Guangxun Wenji*, 290.
28. Ting, *Ding Guangxun Wenji*, 108.

gained respect in that Christianity can now serve the wellbeing of the nation. And of course the re-introduction of the policy of freedom of religion has given a fertile soil for growth.[29]

The overseas conservative wing sees the it differently. The Tertullian quote: 'The blood of the Martyrs is the seed of the Church', is given as the spiritual basis of the surge in numbers. This is seen as Divine sovereignty over a suffering Church. The blood, sweat, tears and prayers of those hard at work have finally bore fruit.

But the reality may be none of the above. A basic survey would give us a very different look to the surge. The fact is that almost eighty per cent of the growth is in rural China, where political agenda has barely touched the less literate and the peasants, and where missionary influence is least evident.[30] If there is any credit due, it was due to the persistent hard work of some older leaders who have kept the flame of their faith glowing, albeit, with great suffering, and always in the precarious situation of petering out. These are the 'uncles' and 'aunties' who went through persecution and endured untold suffering, but have emerged as giants of faith. At work constantly in the most desperate of circumstances in evangelism and pastoral care when not being held in prison or hard labour, which is very frequent, they have managed to reach most

---

29. See for example, Zuo Furong, 'Christianity and Recent Beijing Society', in *Jidujiao yu Jin Xiandai Beijing Shehui* (Sichuan: Bashu Shushe, 2009), 256–77.
30. See a very insightful analysis in the magnum Opus of Leung Kalun, *The Rural Churches of Mainland China Since 1978* (Hong Kong: Alliance Bible Seminary, 1999) [in Chinese].

of the rural regions of China, many of these places have little or no contact with missionaries previously. Two factors stood out for attention. The audacity of these older leaders impart respect and admiration and many see the vibrant faith as very real in the atmosphere of fear and suspicion. And there were report after report of miraculous healing and deliverance through the prayers and teaching of these leaders. Christianity was strange and mostly unheard of to those who witness these phenomena, so most of the converts were new to the faith. Thus teaching in the Christian faith followed in earnest. As a result networks were founded like spider webs that engulf many areas of the inland. These 'uncles' were in great demand, and many took courage from them to embrace a new faith that does not retreat even amidst extreme persecution. They would meet in homes of the host, which served as epicentres of activities around the region; many would travel long distances in order to hear what little they could from the 'uncles'. If there is a true indigenous movement, this is it. It goes without saying that they are very much opposed by the Sstate church.

The dichotomy in the protestant church in the face of it is still influenced by the idea of the so-called house church and the state church, but the boundary is becoming more hazy by the day. The intermingling of the members between these two 'bodies' began in the 1990s. There are several reasons for this. The surge in the number of Christians means that people are gradually defining themselves more as fellow believers and less so with any institutional boundaries. This of course started in the younger generations with carried less 'burden of history'. Meanwhile preaching and pastoring in 'The State Church'[31] have gradually been relaxed in control. Recently, I met with a young pastor of the 'Three-Self church' who felt her responsibility is towards her flock and to be faithful to the Christian message. She was in fact encouraged to do so by the higher authorities. She indicated that this is the trend now, especially with the younger pastors. Although there are no evangelistic revival meetings as such, people are indeed converted in the open church by the hundreds as well. She was saying that dialogue between the 'Three-Self' church and the house churches has already begun in earnest in her area, which has experienced unprecedented growth.

Having said that, entrenched mutual suspicion is still prominent between the state church and the house church. The figures of Wang Mingdao and KH Ting still loom large especially in the theological landscape. They represent the conservative and the liberal wings, even if it is in name only.

Ting is now retired, and although he still exerts some influence,[32] the younger generation of eclectic leaders have already made their positions felt. The hardcore socialist line is still very much in evidence, but as the num-

---

31. I use the term the 'State Church', the 'Open Church' and the 'Three-Self Church' loosely to mean the government registered TSPM and CCA controlled churches, depending on the context of discussion. The overseas Chinese would cautiously use the term 'Open Church'.
32. See his translated work in *A Chinese Contribution to Ecumenical Theology: Selected Writings of Bishop K.H. Ting*, edited by Janice and Philip Wickeri (Geneva: WCC Publications, 2002).

bers adhering to the open church mushroom, some have shown that they are not entirely happy with the status quo. So from both internal re-evaluation of the role of the Three-Self organisation and also the increasingly vigorous contact with the Christian community abroad, the landscape has indeed been shifting. This is very much reflected in the reaction of the Chinese Christian community in the diaspora. Although suspicion of the motive of the Three-Self church is still much discussed, the hardcore disdain of it is slowly but surely eroding. Many join in the worship in the open church while they are home visiting.

Much is said about the 'fundamentalist' outlook of the rural church and the TSPM often cited this as the reason for stamping it down. Some would put down the phenomena of miraculous healings, exorcisms etc to the influence of syncretic folk religious traditions.[33] But this would make a mockery of the New Testament record of the ministry and work of Jesus and the early church. To the rural Chinese church, which was deprived of any proper contact with the wider Christian community, the remarkable surge in the growth in numbers has its roots in precisely these miraculous phenomena. Cases after cases are reported of the great reawakening in rural communities, due to some persons experiencing miracles in their midst.[34] The rural church could pride itself in going back to the New Testament mode of being church. We can almost say with con-

---

33. See, for example, Philip L Wickeri, *Reconstructing Christianity In China: KH Ting and The Chinese Church* (NY: Orbis Books, 2007), 341. Wickeri is typical of scholars who are critical of the phenomena.

34. Cf Tony Lambert, *The Resurrection of the Chinese Church* (London: Hodder & Stoughton, 1991).

fidence that save for the sacrificial sufferings of the leaders, which serve as inspiration of a vibrant belief, miracles are the stimulus for 'Christian fervour' in rural China. Of course there is always the danger of sectarianism and cultism, but the rural church leaders are well aware of false teachings and false experiences that evolve into heresy. Indeed one of the major works that is done to curb heresy is to teach orthodox doctrines. There is constant surveillance towards anybody who comes to their midst with no prior approval from the leaders. Nevertheless, even with due diligence, some still fall into the traps of individual leaders who teach different doctrine and extreme practices. The advent of Falun Gong in China has been denounced by both sides of the church. The rural church is aware of its vulnerability to heretical teachings; it does not find the liberal teachings of the state church any better. Better to be labelled 'fundamentalist' than to compromise the teaching of the Bible.

The call to be faithful to the teaching of the Bible is heard throughout the world. Many overseas Chinese respond, in the hundreds, by assisting in providing teachers on a short-term, intensive basis, mainly on Bible teaching and some theological courses, but they are all very careful not to touch on any sensitive issues pertaining to the church in China. The Chinese protestant church has entered the modern age in that the most recent technologies are being utilised to obtain support material for teaching and training. The latest publications in Chinese are available almost immediately. In fact many believers have no lack of the latest information on the global church. Networking among the younger leaders is vibrant and there is now a sense of community throughout China, which was unheard of even as recently as twenty years ago. A younger generation is slowly taking over the helm of nurturing. Quite a few have now found their way into overseas seminaries in preparation to serve. The TSPM church has also been actively sending personnel overseas to gain higher degrees in order to meet the increasing demand of congregations which are becoming more and more intellectually based, especially in the coastal cities and also where growth is most phenomenal.

Almost as phenomenal is the shift in the attitude of academy towards all things Christian. The open and reform policy has opened up research in all areas of the humanities, under the rubric of social science and philosophy. Academia soon found strong links between western philosophy and Christianity. In the earlier stage of research, some voiced the dependence of the progress of the West on its strong Christian heritage, thus view Christianity in a very positive light. Thus we come full circle to the attitude adopted by the intelligentsia of the 1920s. Although this view has been dampened somewhat with more research into the decline of the West and the secularisation of society into a market-driven economy, the study of Christian thought and philosophy seems to remain a much sought after field. Publications of the research by university philosophy professors are now in abundance, ranging from church history, Enlightenment thought, and modern theologians to patristic thought, especially Augustine. Recently, there is a growing interest in biblical studies, due in part to the realisation that Christian thought and theology must find their root in the Bible. Courses in religion departments in universities have begun to include 'Introduction to the Bible', 'Biblical Theology' and 'Exegesis'; notable among them are the courses offered at Peking University.[35] Although some of the authors and researchers have a Christian background, most enter research purely from great interest in the field. This has given rise to the hot topic of the so-called 'Cultural Christian'.

According to Zhou Xin Ping, the term 'Cultural Christian' was first coined by Bishop Ting in the 1980s to express his welcome to such intellectual research on Christianity and his active attitude towards mutual dialogue and understanding'.[36] But the debate on this uniquely Chinese phenomenon came to a head in the reaction of Christian scholars overseas, in particular in Hong Kong.[37] 1998 saw Bishop Ting in his most persuasive mode, urging the Protestant leadership to resolve on strengthening 'theological reconstruction' in the Chinese church.[38] The program was to see Christian theology in the service of socialist society. The fierce debate that followed was predictable, with each side accusing the other of harbouring hidden agendas.[39]

---

35. Peking University has now offered courses in Introduction to the 'Old and New Testament', 'Biblical Theology', 'Exegesis' on 'Individual Books of the Bible'.
36. *China and Christianity*, 283.
37. See in particular Josephine Leung, *Cultural Christian: Phenomenon and Argument* (Hong Kong: Institute of Sino-Christian Studies, 1997) [in Chinese].
38. Philip L Wickeri, *Reconstructing Christianity In China* 1, 333–34, 346–56.
39. *Ibid*, 1.

The quarrel as to who owns what or who is the rightful heir to the Christian message has occupied the centre stage of discussions and arguments. Even the label 'Cultural Christian' creates much controversy. It is fashionable to argue that the decline of western Christianity is due mainly to the structural church corrupting the very essence of the Christian message. But for the conservative Christians in China, there is still such a thing as the test for genuine Christianity that lies with its adherence to the church, albeit a not-so-structural one. There is a distinct suspicion of people who profess to be Christian and yet hold disdain towards the church. This comes with substantial historical evidence. The TPSM is put into this category. The majority of the house churches view it as embodying a church-destroying ideology. So when voices that profess to be sympathetic to the Christians ethos are heard outside of the confines of the church, they are viewed with immediate suspicion, especially when these voices tried to claim that the church has got it wrong and only *they* know the true essence of Christianity.

The argument from the conservative wing goes like this. Can you be a Christian without adherence to the church? Yes, and this is a message universally agreed upon, even in the house churches, for some obvious reasons. The church is more mobile under government restrictions, and being a 'church member' does not necessarily mean that you are a Christian: look at the so-called church which corroborate with authorities to persecute their brethren! The test of the pudding is in the eating. How can you profess to be a Christian without adherence to the bare minimum of fellowship with fellow believers.

What sort of theological monstrosity is produced without the heartbeat of living out a visible form of what is advocated?

But the problem must be looked at from the perspective of the Chinese intelligentsia throughout the history of Chinese thought. Religion and the study of religious ideas *did* not belong to any one group that adhered to one institution of religious practise. This has been the case since the beginning of Chinese religious thought. You do not have to be a Daoist to delve deep into the ethos of Daoism. Religious thought belong to the realm of ideas. Although some would protest over the non-adherents' view of the religious faithful, there were constant interactions between them. And it was the *ethos* in each individual religious idea that gradually built itself into the heart and soul of being Chinese! Christianity is viewed as part of that pool of religious thoughts by academia. And from the face of it, academia's increasing interest in Christian thought is to be welcomed, as they are trying hard to bring some fresh ethos into what they see as a stale moral and ethical situation in China today. In fact they might be, for all intents and purposes, a bridge to the indigenisation of Christianity in the Chinese mind today. Thus lies the dilemma of Chinese Christian theologians: on the one hand there is a fiercely intense hold on the uniqueness of Christianity; on the other, the strong desire to make Christianity relevant to the Chinese, ie to sink into the heart and soul of being Chinese. It is this struggle that it is the core of the debate.

The 'Cultural Christian' debate has now conceded that there are in fact three categories of scholars who show great interest in Christian studies, and each is contributing to the ongoing search for the relevance and deeper theological reflection of Christianity in the Chinese context. Milton Wan, a well respective scholar in Hong Kong has helpfully categorised them as SMSC (Scholars in Mainland China Studying Christianity), CCSS (Cultural Christian Studies Scholars) and CS (Christian Scholars).[40] CCSS and CS are discussed above. Of relevance here is SMSC. Zhou Xinping points out several characteristics of SMSC:

➤ Their appearances coincide with the interest in religious studies in academic institutions in China.

➤ The sensitive issue of religious studies in present day China means that religion is studied under the rubric of 'cultural studies'.

➤ Academic studies at home and abroad in philosophy, history, sociology and literature and the arts brought them into contact with Christianity.

➤ They are not strictly interested in Christian systematic theology per se, but only as it interacts with the fields of humanities and social science.

➤ Therefore, 'the purpose of their research is also not for self-salvation . . . but for the consideration of cultural value and significance of Christianity towards human beings, and of its historic and social function in the development of human society'.[41]

---

40. Wen Wei-yao (Milton Wan), *On the Transformation and Transcendence of Humanity: A Sino-Christian Perspective* (Beijing: Zongjiao Wenhua Chubanshe, 2009) [in Chinese], 165–91.

41. Zhou, 'Cultural Christians', 286.

Zhou is more positive in his evaluation of the academic study of Christianity. He points out that,

> [t]he phenomenon shows a positive and optimistic atmosphere for understanding and accepting Christianity in the Chinese mainland . . . Their research results and suggestions have been accepted to a greater extent by the government for the improvement of Christian existence and development in contemporary China. They helped to build a bridge between government and religious circles for mutual understanding and exchange.[42]

He is able to see the contribution both in the contextualisation of Chinese theology and the role Christianity can play in the modernisation of China.[43] Although his comments are premature and over optimistic, they do show the earnestness of the appeal for acceptance both inside and outside the church.

Protestant church leaders and theologians have been at work on the contextualisation of Christian theology for quite some time. It was left to overseas Chinese theologians to carry on the research before the government open-door policy. Scholars, both in Hong Kong and Taiwan, have produced much literature on the topic of indigenisation of Christian theology. Much is based on either the interaction of Christian symbols with Chinese

---

42. Zhou, 'Cultural Christians', 298; this comes from a person who is on the inside circle of the phenomenon.
43. Zhou, 'Cultural Christians', 299–300.

indigenous religious beliefs or Christian theology in the Chinese context, with varied degrees of success. But the surge of the number of believers in mainland China has changed all that; at least the whole paradigm of investigation is shifting toward the understanding of the phenomenon and the consequent effect it has on the social fabric of China today.

Fuk-tsang Ying, in his article[44] chronicles the still-sensitive matter of church-state relations, calling this 'Mutual Adaptation to Socialism'. That mutual adaptation comes in two categories: patriotism and positive contribution towards the construction of socialist modernisation.[45] Under the current state of affairs, religion does indeed help to foster a harmonious society, the present CCP slogan. Ying gives a succinct summary of the situation:

> In sum, pragmatism has become the core of the Party-State's policy on religion; they have recognized that religion has a positive social function and are actively inducing it to serve the interests of the Party-State and promote social stability and unity, to advance economic development, and even to consolidate the Party's authority. But on the other hand, at the same time as affirming the positive function

44. Fuk-tsang Ying, 'Mutual Adaptation to Socialism: TSPM and Church-State Relations', in *China and Christianity*, *Concilium*, 2008/2.
45. Ying, 'Mutual Adaptation', 72–74.

of religion, the Party-State also maintains its administrative control over religion.[46]

What this all means for Chinese theological reconstruction (the popularly called Sino-Christian theology), is a narrow alley of movement of thoughts. Chin Ken Pa, a Christian philosopher from Taiwan, in a paper read at the Third Chinese Theology Round Table Conference in Kunming, China in 2005, sees this narrow alley as Christianity being relegated to a religion of ethics and morality.[47] Chin is adamant that the uniqueness of the Christian message lies in its 'otherness'. In this, he is very vocal and set the tone for future dialogue in the search for the soul of the Chinese protestant church:

---

46. Ying, 'Mutual Adaptation', 83.
47. Chin Ken Pa, 'What is "Sino-Christian Theology"?: Third Chinese Theology Round Table Conference, Kunming, 18–23 September 2005', in *China and Christianity, Concilium*, 2008/2: 88–102. We cannot here go into the discussion of Sino-Christian theological construction due to space and also because the enterprise is still ongoing and no consensus or mature work has as yet come to light. The loudest advocate, Liu Xiaofeng, has written substantially of the methodology, but he too finds no strong agreement amongst the scholars. However, he said the following should be taken to heart: 'If the Chinese language itself is unable to break away from the ultimate reality of Confucianism and Daoism, all that 'Sino-Christian theology' has to say remains a contradiction, a kind of impossibility. What Sino-Christian theology needs is a linguistic structure which it can apply to Chinese-language thought so that Chinese-language thought can comprehend the concept of God'; quoted by Chin, 100.

> The Christian religion is basically a 'stumbling block'. To every culture, whether it is Jewish, Greek, European, American, or Latin American culture, Jesus Christ is an 'outsider', and it is for this 'outsider' that Christianity is arguing its case. It is this very 'otherness' that is the attitude in faith that Christian theology must continue to affirm. The great principle to follow when dealing with another culture is to stop trying to be a mediator between cultures, and instead bring about a genuine conversion to the Christian faith.[48]

The way forward is still to remain in cautious dialogue, seeing the protestant church as a positive force in the transformation of humanity under God and the environment in which it lives and moves and has its being.

---

48. Chin, 'What is "Sino-Christian Theology"?', 100.

Contributors

Gianni Criveller, currently based in Hong Kong, has spent 18 years in Greater China: Taiwan, Hong Kong, Macau and the Mainland. He researches, teaches and writes on China and Christianity, with special attention to the reception of Christianity and missionary work and strategies. As researcher at the Holy Spirit Study Centre he observes and comments on the current situation of Catholicism and religious policy in China. Fr Criveller teaches Theology of Mission at the Holy Spirit Seminary College of Philosophy and Theology. He has authored numerous essays and is a priest in the Pontifical Institute of Foreign Missions (PIME).

Claudia Devaux is the author, with the late George Bernard Wong, SJ, of *Bamboo Swaying in the Wind: A Survivor's Story of Faith and Imprisonment in Communist China*. After more than two decades in the high technology industry and one year teaching in Chongqing, she now resides in San Luis Obispo, California, where she does website development and education consulting. She also leads pilgrimages to the Holy Land.

Fr Jeroom Heyndrickx CICM has been a missionary in Taiwan since 1957. In 1982 he founded the Ferdinand Verbiest Institute at the University of Leuven (Belgium), for cooperation and exchange with the Church in China. Since then he has travelled to China several times a year. He is still director of the Verbiest Institute at Leuven and is currently teaching Pastoral Theology at the National Seminary in Beijing.

Roderick O'Brien is a priest and lawyer who has lived and taught in China for some years. He has published a number of articles on religion and ethics in China.

Paul Rule taught Religious Studies at La Trobe University, Melbourne, and remains an honorary associate there. He is currently EDS/Stewart Distinguished Fellow of the Ricci Institute for Chinese/Western Cultural History at the University of San Francisco and a member of the Macau Ricci Institute. He has published widely in Chinese religious history, Aboriginal religion and modern Catholicism.

Fr Benoît Vermander, SJ is director of the Taipei Ricci Institute and chief-editor of www.erenlai.com. He is also consultor to the Pontifical Council for Interreligious Dialogue. Among his recent English-language publications are Olivier Lardinois & Benoit Vermander, eds. *Shamanism and Christianity* Taipei, 2008 and Elise Anne DeVido and Benoit Vermander, eds, *Creeds, Rites and Videotapes, narrating religious experience in East Asia* Taipei, 2004.

Justin Tan is Resident Scholar at the Bible College of Victoria, researching and writing in many areas including Patristics, Christian Spirituality and the Old Testament. He was the first Dean of the Chinese Department in BCV and now also serves as Senior Lecturer there.

Although not born in China, he was brought up in a steeply Chinese tradition, and after becoming a Christian has been interested in Chinese Christianity ever since. He has on many occasions travelled to China to teach and experienced first hand the struggle and growth of the Protestant Church there. He is also visiting Professor in Biblical Studies in one of the top Universities in China.